HAROLD ST. JOHN
A PORTRAIT

by his Daughter
Patricia St. John

I rejoice at Thy word
as one that findeth great spoil.
(Psalm 119:162)

Kingsley Press
Shoals, Indiana

Harold St. John: A Portrait by His Daughter

PUBLISHED BY KINGSLEY PRESS
RR2, Box 43A
Shoals, IN 47581
USA
Tel. (812) 247-3895
www.kingsleypress.com

ISBN: 0-9719983-0-2

Distributed in the United Kingdom by:
Searchlight Literature
P.O. Box 5206
Newark NG23 6YL
England
Tel. (01636) 821322
www.searchlightonline.org

Credits:
Cover sketch by D. Curtis Hale
Graphic design by Edward Cook

Printed in the United States of America

Printed by
Old Paths Tract Society
RR2, Box 43
Shoals, IN 47581

How close we need to keep to God for such a holy ministry, and how soon the bloom wears off. Remember you're a polished shaft, but a breath can spoil the polish.

A sleepless night, but I got my sermon on the floor between three and four in the morning. Preaching is a happy labor, but I must give blood every time.

When I go home, work will begin in eternity the very next morning. Life is not a blind alley; it's a thoroughfare, closing in twilight, opening in dawn.

Contents

Photographs

Publisher's Foreword

THIS book is easily one of the best Christian biographies I have ever read. Somehow it manages to be exciting, inspiring, challenging, amusing and edifying all at the same time. It makes compelling reading from start to finish—hard to put down once you've picked it up.

It was my privilege to meet the author, Patricia St. John, about fifteen years ago. What a charming, gracious, warm-hearted soul she was, full of the joy of living and always abounding in the service of her Saviour. Her wonderful gift as a writer is evidenced by the continuing popularity of her various books, and never was that gift more worthily employed than when she gave to the world the beautiful portrait of her father contained in the following pages. With consummate skill she paints for us an exquisite picture of a radiant saint who dwelt with Christ in the heavenlies, yet who was at the same time eminently human—an earthen vessel full to overflowing with heavenly treasure.

This edition is reprinted from that of 1961 and is the same except for minor revisions in the first and third chapters. These minor revisions have been undertaken by Miss Hazel St. John, Patricia's older sister, who is delighted that the book is being republished. The only other change is that American spelling and punctuation have been used throughout.

We earnestly hope that the perusal of these pages will inspire a new generation of Christians with a burning desire to diligently search the Scriptures as Harold St. John did, never more to be content with surface reading and shallow study of God's holy Word.

Special thanks are due to those who contributed to the costs of printing.

Edward Cook
Kingsley Press
September, 2002

HAROLD ST. JOHN
September 2nd, 1876 to May 11th, 1957

Introduction

IN the churchyard of St. George's village the snowdrops are growing thick in the rough, humpy grass. The ground slopes steeply downward and many of the graves are old and worn, with faded Welsh inscriptions. But on the lowest level is a grave bearing this inscription in English:

HAROLD ST. JOHN
Sept. 2nd 1876 to May 11th 1957
"The beloved of the Lord shall dwell in safety by Him."

The following pages are a record of one who walked from his youth in the conscious joy and dignity of knowing himself "beloved of the Lord." That love captivated him as a very young man and changed the whole course of his life. It energized him with a strength that seemed almost superhuman at times, poured out in a very passion of single purpose; and, at the end, the knowledge of that love grew deeper and brighter, transforming pain and weakness, casting out fear, falling like sunshine on the shadow of death; till as a dying man he could look up radiantly and say, "I am too weak to pray, I am too tired to love Him much, but I'm just lying here, letting Him love me."

Holy growth is subject to fixed laws, and I must obey them—much prayer, true Bible study, full self-control, tight rein on thoughts. These are God's ways for me.

CHAPTER 1

The Child

NOT very much is known of Harold St. John's childhood. His father was Treasurer of Sarawak during the time of Sir Rajah Brooke, so the six children, of whom Harold was the fourth, spent their early years out East. They returned later to Germany and Belgium, where Harold remembers frequently playing truant from school in order to haunt the Brussels picture galleries. One can well imagine him, a sensitive, rather scholarly little boy, with his inherent love of solitude, dreaming among the old masters and grave madonnas, and imbibing some of those strong, lasting impressions that he turned to such account later on. He often based deep lessons on some of those far distant, early impressions, and one to which he loved to refer, dates back to the markets of Sarawak when he was little more than a baby.

"I was a very small boy," he told us once, "and I was coming down the winding passages of an eastern bazaar, a few hundred miles away from Singapore. I was very interested in the various striking things in this bazaar, and I can remember to this day coming to a point where two ways crossed, and there, seated at his work, was a Hindu potter. It's more than fifty years ago, but I can remember him now with his white turban, his keen, piercing eyes and long tapering fingers; at his feet a great disc of stone worked by a treadle, and in his hand a smaller disc of metal revolving swiftly. By his side was a small table and on it lay a lump of damp clay, and ever and anon his long fingers would go into the water, and then they would transfer the clay to the discs spinning so swiftly, with one hand pressing it outside, and the other moulding it inside while there grew in beauty and exquisite shape a vessel to the potter's glory. And I shall never forget the quiver that ran through my childish frame as suddenly a little shiver passed through the clay and the whole piece fell, a shapeless mass, in the potter's hand. He gathered it up swiftly, but the whole thing was so distressing and poignant to me that I turned away, unwilling to look at a thing I did not like. I had no words to describe what I had seen, but I knew there was something I could never un-see. I had seen the whole philosophy of man's earthly life. I had seen power, but, thank God, I dimly saw something other than power that day. I saw the purpose behind the power."

No doubt time lent depth to his infant musings, but the gift of interpretation was certainly given at an early age. He had a vivid memory of being carried, as a very little boy, in a sedan chair up a high mountain in bright sunshine. On one side of the path was a precipice, and he would often tell how the bearer carried him to the edge and bade him look down. Far below over the valley a mighty storm was raging, and as the child gazed down into the grey abyss he realized that he had actually journeyed above the clouds. Below, the hurricane was raging, but he had reached a golden place of peace.

While he was quite small his mother, Blanche St. John had, during one of the family's visits to England, come under the influence of an evangelical mission, believed, and become a new creature. She threw in her lot with the Brethren Movement, and the home was a truly Christian one, with the mother's influence strong and abiding. All her six children grew up to be Christian men and women, and all look back with gratitude to the saintly woman, beautiful in face and character, who brought them up. And in that rather unusual atmosphere of constant travel and change, Harold grew from childhood to boyhood. He was not always happy. The boys in the school he attended in Germany were not always kind to the band of young foreigners in their midst, but they admired him for his physical courage and for his fighting powers, and his love of books made him more self-sufficient than most children. There was also the delight of his father's occasional home-comings. Their father would take his children for prodigiously long walks, on one occasion walking them from London to Oxford—a taste which remained with Harold all his life.

His early dreams were of scholarship—school, college, and the endless delights of study. It all seemed possible, too. The eldest brother had entered a medical school, and the family was comfortably off; a world of learning stretched in front of the eager boy, and in the background of his dreams rose the spires and towers of Oxford. But the dream was short lived. The family was already threatened by severe financial losses when his father died suddenly, out in Mexico.

Very little was left to provide for the widow and the six children, and it must have been a dark time for the mother. But her faith in the heavenly Father's care never wavered; she knew that He would provide, and help was given. The eldest boy was enabled to finish his medical studies, and the eldest girl took a post in the Civil Service. The two middle boys left school, and helpful relatives found work for them in a city office; and in that office those two inwardly rebellious lads turned their backs resolutely on their life's ambitions. Arthur knew that he would never enter the diplomatic service; Harold knew that he would never go to Oxford.

Harold, at that time, had no personal, spiritual refuge, although he outwardly revered his mother's faith; and the high hopes of his life seemed to have been blighted at the outset. But he determined to do what was in his power to become a self-educated man. He read everything he could get hold of and spent most of his spare time browsing in the second hand book shops. The rosy-faced young clerk, with his overcoat pockets bulging with books, became a well-known figure in Paternoster Row. His amazing secular knowledge and wealth of preaching illustrations from geographical, scientific, and historical sources, dated from those hungry years when he craved for learning, defied fate, and helped himself to what life seemed to have denied him.

He got on well; his salary was by no means high, and he helped support the home in Bayswater, London; but he was a clever mathematician, well versed in French and German, and a conscientious, trusted worker and there was plenty of opportunity for rising to a high position if he persevered.

And then, when he was eighteen years old, on the 20th October, 1894, something happened. The circumstances that led up to that night of wrestling and anguish are not known. It was a night so awful and holy that he never spoke of it in detail, and when questioned about it, his answers were evasive. But we know that there wrestled a Man with him till break of day, and that until morning he paced up and down in the dark, or lay on his face before God. But he came through with a vision of Christ which never for one moment grew dim and a faith that never for a moment deserted him for the rest of his life.

"I remember the day—I shall never forget it," he said many years later, "when I saw my Saviour with the giant's head in His hand, unchallengeable proof that the work of salvation was eternally finished, for He had destroyed him that had the power of death, and, through fear of death had imprisoned those who all their lifetime were subject to bondage. And since that day, when I knew my Saviour had destroyed the giant and broken his power for ever, and carried the witness of His victory up to the City of God—since that day, I have never known the slightest challenge or fear in my heart as to my eternal security in the Lord Jesus Christ. I stand before God tonight as having, by faith, seen my Saviour with the marks of His victory. He has triumphed, He has gone up to God, and by His mercy I am going there too."

Like Paul on the Damascus road, he had undergone an experience that made of him a completely new creature. The eager young student with his unsatisfied intellect and restless, far-flung desires, was born again overnight. In his stead stood a young man with a single, undeviating purpose and passion, forced into one single channel of untiring love and action. He could have said in all truth and simplicity,

> *All the vain things that charm me most,*
> *I sacrifice them to His blood.*

And yet the dreams of youth die hard. In the Spring of 1908 he visited Oxford and sauntered round the colleges in the late afternoon, when the April sun lay long on the quadrangles and the borders flamed against the old grey stones. "I betray my restless heart," he wrote in his diary, "by the fierce longing I have for learning. God never gave me the chance, so He does not mean me to have it. Jacob had a ladder to help him to rise up to God, but there is none in the first of John. Christ has taken Jacob's place, and there is no distance between Christ and God in glory."

So he passed the final verdict on his early aspirations—learning is a ladder not to be despised, and he never did despise it, and ensured a good education for all his children. But for him all ladders led but to one destination—"That I may know Him." There, with the old universities weaving their familiar spell around him, he realized with an upward rush of joy that he had by-stepped the ladder. He was a man in Christ, and there is no distance between Christ and God.

CHAPTER 2

The Evangelist

"IS your life a Nile or an Amazon?" Harold St. John once asked his hearers in later years, when lecturing on the secrets of spiritual power.

He had been describing and contrasting the mouths of these two great rivers. The inland Nile is a splendid river, watering the land and carrying ships on its broad flow, but as it nears the coast it divides and subdivides into a wide delta, and where the erstwhile noble river runs into the sea, nothing remains but a great stretch of mud, broken by myriads of sluggish little streams, that stain the vivid blue of the Mediterranean for miles out.

The Amazon is also a broad, noble, inland river, but as it nears the coast the banks become narrower and higher. Its waters are forced through a long rigid channel that concentrates its power into one current, that has no outlet except straight forward. When the river finally bursts out into the Atlantic, the power of that rushing water carries all before it, and ships crossing the mouth of the Amazon must keep away from the shore, or they will capsize.

In the early years after his conversion, Harold St. John's life was an Amazon indeed. Those who knew him later, when that passionate current of self-hatred and ardent desire had lost itself in the ocean of the consciousness of God's love, found it difficult to recognize in the old saint who radiated peace, joy and humour, the almost fanatically ascetic young man who poured out his thoughts and spiritual longings in a diary. But those thoughts ran deep below the surface, and his contemporaries give a less intense picture of him. Mr. Percy O. Ruoff, who worked with him in the bank, recalls him in the following words:

"Looking at the portrait of dear Harold St. John on my desk, taken when he was a young man, purpose, earnestness and guilelessness seem nearly vocal. It brings back his virile early manhood. I can see him, swift as a swallow, with swinging arms like wings, deftly steering his way and never colliding with any, on the thronged pavements of Cheapside, the despair of those who tried to walk with him. He was off to his favorite Paternoster Row, the sanctum of books, or to the Thursday mid-day service to listen to the massive and original Joseph Parker at the City Temple, or to A. E. Stewart, or the Reverend Marcus Rainsford, or to some notable evangelist at the Monday YMCA in Aldersgate Street.

"Never once have I seen Harold dawdle in the street or in life. He always appeared to be urged by some purpose. In the London County Bank in Lombard Street (later the Westminster Bank), which we both joined in 1896, he was just the same, full of movement and vigor. It was too much to expect that with the name of St. John he would escape being affectionately known by all as 'Florrie,' the name of the popular Music Hall artiste of the day. Well known to be a preacher, verbal traps were set to catch him into which he innocently fell, but he always took it in good part and soon became wary of such artful devices.

"Harold, G.S. and myself were dubbed 'the holy trinity' as we sallied forth to a little tuck shop in Birchin Lane. The almost invariable fare consisted of a cold sausage roll and a cup of coffee, totaling 7 pence on the bill. A Spartan diet was imposed on us in those days, because the stern fact of expenditure was seldom absent from the mind, and all our disbursements had to be adjusted to our total income of £70 per annum at this head office.

"Recollections of these early days are vivid. Sitting together on top of the Two Horse Bus going towards Holborn, I was describing open air preaching in North London. Never shall I forget his words, considered in the light of his subsequent preaching. He looked at me and said, 'Whatever do you say to the people listening?' He soon discovered what to say for he always outstripped the lot of us, who, after a frugal tea at the A.B.C., went to the Mile End Waste to preach every Friday evening. St. John with his powerful voice and fluent tongue drew and held the crowds with his graphic word pictures and his youthful, ruddy appearance. Either alone or with one other he would go to Hyde Park and preach to the crowds.

"A word or two more before passing from his banking career, which extended nearly twenty years, to his personal qualities. He was quite the most popular man at the Bank, always cheerful and bright, although the butt and target for friendly thrust and banter. Never did I hear him speak a bitter or reproachful word, although often provoked. It was a usual thing with him to shoulder extra work and enable a colleague to get away a bit earlier. As often as possible he would rush to the British Museum after Bank House hours and lay hand on a variety of treasures for future preaching. Maybe one Saturday afternoon he would board a train for Newcastle, take meetings, snatching sleep on the return train journey, and would appear on Monday morning for business, fresh as a daisy. Always on the go, doing the work of two men, leaving the impression that he recognized that the King's business requires haste."

The Bank Manager wrote of him about fifty years later:

"I often wonder at the way St. John changed the whole tone of 21 Lombard Street office from evil talk, swearing and bad behavior, to good behavior. Harold used to speak with almost every man he worked with about the things of God, and a number responded favorably." His arrival at the Bank was a red letter day for one of the young Christian clerks, E. G. Wanhill, who became his life-long friend. "Early in 1896," he writes, "the chief clerk of the London County Bank, 21 Lombard Street, London, called me to his desk and introduced me to a rosy-faced young man, Harold St. John, a newcomer to that office, and told me to show him where to hang up his hat and coat. In the course of our conversation, we both had the joy of finding ourselves to be born-again Christians, Harold some two years previously, myself only a few months. Harold, a keen, brainy young man, was one of a family of Brethren and that, added to his literally devouring the Word of God, made him an able teacher and help, in spiritual matters, to my comparatively ignorant self. What a privilege was mine! We often had lunch together or visited Paternoster Row or strolled along the embankment, our conversation being about God, His Word, His grace. Our hearts burned as He walked with us and we hungered and thirsted after the living God with a love so intense that at times it was a positive pain. Harold never had time for sport or ordinary pastimes. His whole being hungered after the living God and the preaching of the gospel of Jesus Christ, and in the open air and in missions many sought his personal help to find the Saviour."

These are the memories of old men looking back over nearly sixty years. One adds, "I am 86 now; my own frame is very weary," but to each the figure of Harold St. John stands out clear and definite, undimmed by the mists of time. His personality and ministry were unforgettable. An old saint in a small Welsh Gospel Hall heard the name, and his face lit up—"I knew him long before he was married," he said. "It must have been over fifty-eight years ago. He held meetings in a granary at Burton-on-Trent. He preached on the flood. Never, never have I forgotten those messages."

These testimonies of blessing received in the early years of Harold St. John's ministry could be multiplied indefinitely. But what of the man? A faded old diary gives something of the soul-searching, passionate loneliness and love of those early years. There is no trace of pride or consciousness of success in the intimate, scribbled records of the young man's spiritual hunger and thirst—no echo in his own heart of the love and esteem in which he was beginning to be held by so many. His first love for Christ showed itself in evangelistic zeal and a longing for souls.

Jan. 2   Preached at Horsham. No liberty.

Jan. 8   Hall full and prayer meeting after. Is revival beginning? O God, give me purpose in prayer. Guard my lips from folly and open them for testimony.

Jan. 15   Hall full, but, oh for power! True teaching and natural freedom useless. Why is it withheld? More prayer and obedience to the will of God. A watch tells time if in harmony with the universe.

Jan. 29   Hall well filled. By grace some power, but it is not revival. Oh, let it come; my heart breaks for it. I haven't begun to live the Christian life. I need ways directed by the Word and sympathies in harmony with the mind of Christ.

Feb. 24   Spent all night in prayer with M.G. Preaching next day, voice failed and spirit too. Wonderful stories of revival in Wales. Why not here?

But in April, 1905, he saw those early prayers for spectacular revival power answered in a very real way. He spent his Easter holidays, as he spent nearly all his holidays, conducting a series of meetings. He and his elder brother, Arthur, traveled down to the little fishing town of St. Ives, in Cornwall, to hold an evangelistic campaign. Those meetings were remembered throughout the lifetime of many of the fishermen of St. Ives. Thirty-five years later Harold St. John's daughter visited the town and walked along the shore where old fishermen were mending their nets. She was surprised at the stir of interest as the news circulated—Harry's daughter has come. Weatherbeaten, wrinkled faces broke into smiles, and some came forward to clasp her hand. The girl's face had revived old memories of the days when two young men had preached night after night in the power of the Spirit, and of the revival fire which spread in the town.

One who was a young woman at the time still recalls that week:

"Looking back over the long years, one can still remember the feeling of being in the presence of God—one's own unworthiness, but the utter worthiness of the Lord Jesus Christ. The after-meetings were times of great blessing—very large numbers responded to the invitation and many were saved.

"One particular night John Newton's hymn was sung:

> *In evil long I took delight*
> *Unawed by shame or fear,*
> *Till a new object struck my sight*
> *And stopped my mad career.*
> *Oh, the Lamb, the spotless Lamb,*
> *The Lamb on Calvary,*
> *The Lamb that was slain, Who liveth again,*
> *To intercede for me.*

"There was no undue excitement, but again and again that chorus was sung with real worship."

The little diary is packed with joyful incident.

9th   A packed hall; two cases of conversion.

10th   L. came in drunk, but sobered down in the middle, and cried out, "Jesus Christ has saved me in this hall."

11th   Crowds at the first meeting. Fifty more came in at 9:30. Five cases of conversion. Left the hall at 11:00. I sorely need wisdom to direct.

13th   Five to ten cases of conversion. I spoke on 1 Corinthians 14:34.

Rowdyism in the meeting. Stayed till midnight with backsliders. Two young men confessed grandly. One dropped down on the floor crying, "If that's the gospel, I accept Christ."

14th   T.C. broke down and came out well for Christ. A fine brothers' meeting re converts. Several more till midnight. Beginning of real opposition.

15th Sunday   Five received at the Lord's Table. An overflowing meeting. One stood and confessed as he took the bread. Three gospel meetings in the evening. Brethren praying up above, and the rest of us jammed out down below. Twelve to thirteen cases of real blessing.

Monday   Backslider brought fellow servant, who, after reading Romans 10:9 over a hundred times, rose and said, "I'm saved." Another young woman came out with, "I believe it, I've got it." Asked prayer for C.C. at 9:00 p.m. At 9:20 p.m., he rose and confessed. Finished at 11:45 p.m.

Tuesday   Here I was denounced at the Chapel as an imposter, sending people to hell. Good, I'd like to meet Mr. D! Full meeting, but slack on judgment and hell. Lack of power leads to heart searching.

Wednesday   Reaping day. Nine cases of conversion. One said, "I needn't go upstairs, I received Christ here."

Thursday   Landlord of the Inn closed his pub, saying, "I can't serve God in this business."

Friday   Huge overflow; many turned away.

Sunday   Finished by 11:00 p.m. after 11 hours' meeting.

Monday   On all day. One old man prayed, "Lord, make me happy and comfortable all day."

A crowd of 300 saw him off at the station, when he went back to London. Perhaps the sea had never seemed so blue before as the train journeyed up the Cornish coast. He had tasted the sweetness of seeing souls in large numbers brought into Christ's kingdom; he had felt the breath of revival power in the very way he had prayed and yearned for it. But as far as we can tell he did not pray quite like that again, nor did he again see large, spectacular ingatherings of newly saved souls. Perhaps he was expressing his new trend of thought in the quiet words: "I sorely need wisdom to direct," for gradually he was turning from the more rewarding work of the revival evangelist to the deep, patient task of the teacher who builds up the converts in the Faith and in the Word.

He lodged that night in a shop. "A good all-night of prayer, 11:00-5:30," reads the diary, "Then slept on the counter before going back to work." Harold St. John's holiday was over.

He never forgot that early experience of mass soul-winning, nor did he undervalue it, but he was alive to its dangers unless allied with subsequent solid Bible teaching. He could never really rejoice over showy results unless certain of their depth and lasting reality. And this love of depth and solidity drew him inevitably towards his great life-work of student, teacher and expositor. But the way was not yet clear and he questioned the change in himself. "A subtle something hinders. Again no one saved. Crowds and liberty, but I come away depressed because of no results. I ought to see them. I am not successful as an evangelist; teaching comes happily."

And then gradually the quiet realization that all was well. "I shall need power tomorrow and must cast out Satan first. Christ can. Weary after four meetings. No fire, but I believe grace and truth were told out, and the day will tell."

Yet in spite of increasing hours given to study and teaching, he still longed to preach the gospel to every creature and spent hours distributing tracts and visiting the slums. His heart ached over the poor prostitute in the park to whom he gave a Gospel. "Is it a bad book?" she asked. "No, it is a good book about Christ," he answered. "Then I can't take it. I have to earn my living," she replied. And thrusting it back into his hand she hurried away, leaving him in anguish.

Night after night he preached in the open air, or in lodging houses, or helped Miss Ada Habershon in her work among the down and outs. He was deeply troubled at first with the callous indifference of these poor men to his message. But later he loved to tell how he himself had ultimately found the way to bridge the gap and learned a lesson that colored all his future ministry.

"When I was quite young I used to go down to the slums of London. I would go into a common lodging house on a Sunday night dressed in a frock coat and a silk top hat and I would stand there with a Testament in my hand and preach and preach, and be very much surprised that the people did not listen to me. I was enormously impressed at their iniquity! Here was a young man in a frock coat and a silk top hat, and they didn't even listen to him! Then I discovered the reason *why* they would not listen, and I got hold of the oldest suit I could borrow and in the pocket of that suit I placed the sum of 4 pence, and in the evening I went, with the rag-tag and bobtail of the district, to that lodging house where two or three hundred men were to sleep for the night. I sat where they sat, and the fleas that bit them bit me; and the same crawly things that crawled on them crawled on me. I spent some nights in that dreadful chamber silently listening to their needs and woes. Then at six o'clock one morning when they were getting their breakfast, I arose and began to speak to them, and now I found there was not the slightest difficulty in obtaining their attention. I had sat where they sat, generally for about nine wakeful hours, and I understood exactly how dirty they were, how the seas of life were buffeting them, and they were perfectly willing to listen to a man who had sat where they sat. And the greatest day in our history was the day when it came to the heart of God to draw closer to us than He had ever done before. After forty centuries of dwelling in cloud and thick darkness, it came to the heart of God to come closer to us. But He did not send His Son to start preaching some code: when our Lord went into the business of Redemption, for thirty years He never said a word of public ministry. For thirty years He sat where men sat and learned their thoughts and experiences. For thirty years He knew hunger, weariness, poverty, and the shadows and cares of that little home, and when He had learned all these things, then He opened His mouth and began to speak. And the world has been listening ever since."

He could look back in kindly, mellowed wisdom, and could laugh a little at the earnest, indignant young man in the silk top hat, but he didn't laugh much at the time. Constant traveling, sleepless nights spent in prayer or late hours of study often left him weak and tired. It did not, however, seem to have occurred to him that he might have slackened the pace.

Aug. 1905   Heavy cold, but some liberty at night. I am ashamed to allow an earthen vessel to hinder. Up at 4:30. Busy week of engagements, but not much spiritual power. Oh, if I am declining, let me die sooner than live and dishonor Christ.

Jan. 1906   Collapsed with temperature of 101. Commanded to rest. A good day in bed. I learn much in sickness. Memorized Psalm 107. A time of power. Bad abscess and neuralgia, but we learn to place our trials in connection with the rest of Christ.

He recalls that he allowed his sister's baby to jump on his chest when he was ill, but it seems to have been the only form of relaxation he considered permissible in sickness. Mental relaxation he condemned utterly in those stern young days.

Feb. 6   Neuralgia awful but grace tells its tale. Up all night but happy with thoughts of the Word.
Feb. 7   Read rubbish till 2:0 a.m. Could I believe such animal folly when I am waiting for Him?

At the end of 1906 he had probably realized the direction of his life's work and the entries in his diary show a more integrated conflict. On New Year's Eve he looked back over the strenuous year like a spent runner who pauses before girding himself for the next lap.

Reviewing 1906 he wrote, "Much to praise for. Blessing to unsaved souls comparatively small, but believers appear to have been helped. I need to watch personal luxury and carelessness of speech. This is more than a little fly in the ointment. What may not 1907 bring? It must give me Christ's grace and care as I have never, never yet known them."

CHAPTER 3

A Workman Approved Unto God

For ah! the Master is so fair
His smile so sweet to banished men,
That they who glimpse Him unaware
Can never rest on earth again.

And they who see Him risen far
At God's right hand to welcome them
Forgetful stand of home and land
Desiring fair Jerusalem.

"MR. ST. JOHN," said a lady, coming up to him at the close of a meeting, "I would give the world to know the Bible as you do."

"Madam," replied the young preacher with a courteous little bow, "that is exactly what it costs."

The world had nothing to say to Harold St. John in those days of young intensity, and he seems to have mistrusted even its most innocent recreations; he does record a visit to the Zoo, but he seems to have gone with a spirit fore-armed against any slackening!

"Went to the Zoo. Saw much of God's handiwork. Greatly enjoyed it all but tried to practise perambulatory prayer. It helps to keep the windows of the soul closed to all around."

He had not yet learned to link life's recreations with the God Who gives us all things richly to enjoy. The banks were still deep and narrow, and natural pleasure at that point seemed a form of temptation.

"A light heart hinders my gravity. How I long to walk with Him. A sleepy, poor reading, a great romp with the children. Perhaps this hinders. I am a lonely man."

He seemed at this point to condemn secular reading, but it was a constant struggle to keep away from it. "Praise and blame are outside

my path. It is Christ I must walk with. My snares are reading and foolish talk. I am called to walk with God. I feel I am playing with divine
things. I need to keep balanced as to life's sorrows."

"My body is Christ's home—a solemn, thrilling sentence. It made
me clean something unsuitable off the bookshelf and sent me to my
knees. Shall I not give Him the last keys of the house?"

He was setting up a rigid scaffolding for his future life, and he
never for himself forsook that early austerity and self-discipline. He
struggled to acquire it, and as a young man he was intensely conscious
of the struggle; but later it became habitual and the whole edifice so
suffused with the light of love and joy that the scaffolding became
invisible. In fact it is difficult to recognize in the ascetic young man
the father who later on marched into a café accompanied by a hungry
schoolgirl daughter he was meeting and, carried away by the delight of
the reunion, astonished the waitress by asking for "the largest and best
ice-cream you have in the shop." Right to the end, beneath his large-
hearted generosity and general enjoyment of life, there beat the heart
of a Nazarite.

In 1906 he wrote: "My birthday today—what a 10 years! I clearly
see my greatest snare—personal luxury. Not excess, but luxury. Paul
kept the rein upon himself and so conquered and became God's man.
God presses this on me. Ease and comfort is drifting work, and I must
not go downstream."

Looking back over a lifetime of rigid self-discipline he sounded
out a clarion call in some of his last lectures on 1 Corinthians 9. "Now
to make quite sure of this business," says Paul, "I am going to do two
things. First, I'm going to be a racer, with his eyes on the tape, and every bodily desire and form of freedom that might make it hard to win
the race is going to be surrendered. And, secondly, like a boxer standing
in the ring, with every muscle ready to rain his blows on the other man,
I take this body, the vessel in which I am prepared to serve Christ, and
beat it black and blue to keep it ready.

"In these days of self-indulgence and easy living and high standards of comfort, do you suppose there are no Christians entrapped
and weakened by the appetites such as eating and drinking and similar
things? Are there none who put family and wife and child before the

interests of the Lord Jesus? Are there none cursed with covetousness, and to whom the lure of gold may become a permanent, evil thing? I keep under my body, lest having preached to others I myself might be a castaway."

The use of his holidays seems to have worried him. They were usually spent on the Continent, giving away tracts or visiting meetings. He looked forward to them with trepidation, his pleasure clouded by the fear of wasting time or relaxing.

"My continental trip will want much grace and much prayer. Evil waxes powerful, *but God!*—how rich to know His love—how it fences me round."

Though recreation and travel proved powerless to satisfy that burning young heart, he had his own joy. Often at this time it was eclipsed by the sense of his own unworthiness and the thirst of his aspirations. But it was a joy so real and deep that he was sometimes almost overwhelmed by it. And all his life it made him in some ways a completely self-contained man, apparently quite independent of his circumstances.

"Work daily gives more joy. Oh, what a Master is Christ! How is it all don't love Him?"

"The final use of redemption is the reputation of God. God has made me a happy man. I worship Him for it."

"Studied the Word. Perhaps the best two evenings I have ever spent—almost too much joy in the Lord. Simply fagged out, but happy with the sense of His love. I can count on Christ every step of the way."

"I was never freer or happier in my life. I can at least feed His sheep in perplexing days. Nowhere is rest but in Him and His love and His service. Wonderful meeting on Samson's death."

"These are my sweetest times. The Word tastes marvelously fresh and glows in my heart. Fine time in train over God's silent love. Nearly broke down at the table, overwhelmed with Christ's love."

More and more the study and the ministry of the Word were becoming the passion of his life. Young as he was he was beginning to be talked about as a Bible teacher of no ordinary merit, and he was taking part in the weekly meetings for employees, held in the big London stores such as Whiteley's and Shoolbred's, and assisting Lord Radstock in his well known drawing-room meetings. In spite of a 9-hour working day he seldom had an evening free from preaching engagements, sometimes in London, sometimes much further afield.

A lady in Sheffield has recalled some of these weekend visits, when Harold St. John would board the afternoon train and arrive in time for the Saturday evening meeting.

"Weekend after weekend for months on end and at other times, Mr. St. John sacrificed much for Sheffield. It was in the days before tape recorders or general knowledge of shorthand, but a group of us used to take notes, and by comparing them we could practically reconstruct the lectures. These notebooks are still consulted, and perhaps the greatest part of his life work has been to give a love of Bible study and the thirst to learn Greek to hundreds and hundreds of young people to whom he has been a father in Christ. Mr. St. John would take a train from London and go direct to the prayer meeting which preceded the address on a Saturday evening. On one occasion we feared he had missed the train, but a search found him in the downstairs schoolroom, stretched out on a table in agonizing prayer. After speaking on Saturday evening, Sunday morning, Sunday School, an Open Air Meeting at 3:15 and a Gospel Meeting, as well as leading eager discussions around dinner and tea table, he would catch the midnight train to London and sleep in the station waiting-room until time to go back to the Bank on Monday morning."

His Bible notes must have covered thousands of loose sheets which he kept in perfect order. He would work through a book at a time, giving a series of lectures on it at different meetings. The study was pure sweetness to his eager intellect and hungry heart, but he agonized over his lectures. He criticized his own style ruthlessly, subjected himself to a searing self-examination. He judged himself before God and was never for one moment carried away or deceived by the applause or approval of his audience.

"Packed meeting. Arrived home 7:00 a.m. I fear I haven't enough sense of the holiness of the Lord's presence and am not sensitive to spiritual direction. I need to help souls, not merely preach."

"A full day, but lack the fullness of the Spirit, and confess it as sin. I have tried to display too much. My object must be Christ alone, not a fine sermon. Cheap to a degree."

"Poor word given in haste at the Morning Meeting. It never pays to be in a hurry in His presence. If others play Jack-in-the-Box—don't you! Lack of prayer prevents power. When shall I learn this lesson? The work of prayer grows on me—Oh to practise it."

"Old sermons won't do. I must work out fresh outlines. There is plenty in the Word, but my mind is a perfect jungle, ignorant, superficial. Not so many as before—my style drives the young away. Too demanding and above their heads. I need to be more simply presenting Christ."

"A bad day. Packed overflow meeting but all flat. I can't lecture on the Lord's coming, I don't live it enough. I was wrong in soul, away and out of touch. Got home heartily humiliated, though everybody else delighted with the meeting."

"One and a half hours after-meeting to a crowd of young men. I drove them all away, because I could not hold them. O faithless servant, but what a Master!"

"A dispiriting lecture to a handful of resigned looking people. London is a freezing place spiritually."

But although he was quick to recognize his faults and deplore the difficulty he found in the need of keeping his soaring thoughts within the boundaries of the average intellect, he could not fail to see that God was blessing, and he occasionally notes this with a sort of surprised humility. "If I was a man of greater grace and zeal, this would be my life's work—holy, living preaching. What a broken reed I am, yet souls seem to heed. Spiritual power increases and I think souls are getting blessed."

"Lectured six or seven times. Preached the best sermon I ever preached. Certainly it was not by human power."

"Taking stock shows weakened spiritual fiber and retrogression as my two besetting sins. This is to myself, but how fair and near Christ has been, and how wonderful. He used my ineffective ministry. Only a great artist could work with such a broken, worthless tool, and yet achieve. Grace, grace unto the headstone. I long to meet my Lord."

There are glimpses, too, in this diary of the seriousness of his preparation. His preaching was not due to any facile oratory or intellectual grasp. It was the result of communion with God and careful self-preparation.

"Has Christ a branch in me through which He can express Himself?" he once asked, and he realized increasingly that blessing depended on abiding in Christ and the spiritual warfare of prayer against the powers of darkness.

"A sleepless night, but I got my sermon on the floor between three and four in the morning. Preaching is a happy labour, but I must give blood every time. A fearful month's work lies ahead and I must pray a great deal. I am clumsy, unaccustomed to His easy yoke. Jacob's lesson must still be mine—he prevailed. Will He give me what I want—power with the angel?"

He knew that depression and discouragement could be crippling, and he was constantly on the guard against them.

"God has called me to admire the love of Christ. I am kept from grovelling by that. I may not despair of even a cinder heap of life. The tendency to depression must be resisted. These are testing days and Christ is more than life; He never disappoints the heart, and I am linked to a risen Man."

He knew, too, the need of keeping himself and disciplining himself for the ministry, an instrument ready and fit for the Master's use.

"How close we need to keep to God for such a holy ministry, and how soon the bloom wears off. Remember you're a polished shaft, but a breath can spoil the polish. Holy growth is subject to fixed laws, and I must obey them—much prayer, true Bible study, full self-control, tight rein on thoughts. These are God's ways for me."

"Christ calls loudly for devotedness, and I must awake and put on my beautiful garments and work, for the night is coming. My life seems bounded by four verbs—am, ought, will, can. Am I wasting my life in half devotion and half worldliness? I long to be out and out for Christ. Asa did well in his youth but wasted later years. Am I like that?"

The Clarendon Room assembly has been described as follows: "The assembly at Clarendon Room, Notting Hill, London, where Harold St. John had his first spiritual home, had a distinctive atmosphere. Associated with it at various times were such notable people as the elderly Countess of whom he spoke in one of his addresses towards the end of his life, Colonel Wellesley, a close relative of the Iron Duke, and Mr. James F. Hamilton, a most dignified and gracious personage, who was Secretary of Coutts Bank from 1906 until his death in 1915. Mrs. St. John writes that, as she looks back, she feels that the writer of the Epistle of James would have approved of the spirit there. There was, for instance, no familiarity between the people who represented different classes of the society of those days, but there was an absolute oneness in Christ and brotherly love.

"Harold's mother ran the women's meeting, helped by her elder daughter, Ella. All the family had Sunday School classes at various times. A boy once asked Evelyn, the youngest brother, 'Are you the St. John of the Bible?' . . . 'Oh, I always thought you were.' Classes were held for boys in the evenings by Harold's sister Ella, where she taught them handicrafts. She was a saintly woman. There would be a pew full of deaf and dumb people at the Sunday morning gathering, and old Mrs. Schofield translated for them—a great attraction to the young-sters present at the meeting. Harold used to translate for them when Mrs. Schofield was absent; his brother Arthur could do this too.

"During the winter weather there were monthly Bible readings, when an address would be given followed by questions. The place would then be full, people coming from other parts of London, and tea would be provided. Mr. W. J. Lowe very often gave the monthly ad-dresses. He was a great friend of Mr. Swain and often stayed with him during Mrs. St. John's childhood. He was a very lovable, gentle man, with a delightful twinkle in his eye, and a very real scholar. He would frequently minister in French among the 'Darbyists' on the Continent and was deeply loved in Switzerland. He seemed, to young Ella Swain, to bear a resemblance to Elisha.

"Harold used to have Bible studies for young men, not at the meeting but in his mother's home. Everyone went to the weekly prayer meeting and Bible reading at Clarendon Room. There were open-air meetings, and lodging houses were visited and tracts distributed. The situation of the hall was just in the right district, on one side, for Sunday School work and women's meeting work, and the Sunday School flourished."

Harold gained much by the company, advice and criticism of older, more mature Christians, one or two of whom he counted his fathers in Christ. Yet he held firmly to his own individuality and refused to copy the style of those he considered his superiors in the ministry. Speaking of two of his greatest friends he wrote:

"I may and do heartily admire them and thank God who has carried both so far beyond me. But I must learn to speak only what I have really enjoyed with God. He denies no creative faculty."

Yet there were also discouragements, and the year 1909 was one of conflicting opinions and real disagreements among those he most respected; something which caused him much unhappiness. He brought his perplexities to the light of God's Word and took his stand once for all on the side of tolerance, personal humility and broad charity in so far as they were compatible with basic doctrinal truth.

And as the stormy year drew to a close, he could look back from a vantage point of peace. "Christ and I have been through this year together," he wrote. "Thank God no cloud rests upon my title to enjoy a Father's love."

CHAPTER 4

The Lover

When you were in your teens, lad, and I was only three,
Oh, then we played at piggy-back, as gay as gay could be.
So ho! for the joy of childhood years, and my love will always be
With the boy who played at piggy-back with a curly maid of three.

When you were in your twenties, and I was seventeen,
By lake and mountainside we roamed like any king and queen;
So ho! for the joy of girlhood days, and my dearest friend has been
The man who climbed the hills with me when I was seventeen.

When you were in the thirties, and I was twenty-three,
A lover bold you came along and stole my heart from me.
So ho! for the joy of courting days, and my love will ever be
With the man who gave me all his heart, when I was twenty-three.

Now you are in your forties, and I am growing staid,
Once more you play at piggy-back with a little curly maid;
So ho! for the joy of man and wife, and my whole life's love will be
With the man who played at piggy-back with Hazel, and with me.

And now today's our wedding day, the years have run to three,
And I send this rhyme with all my love for the years that still shall be,
And Hazel sends a kiss, my dear, and Farnham, Oh so wee,
Can only send a dream, my dear, as he's fast asleep by me.

Lines written by his wife on their
third wedding anniversary, July, 1917

WHEN Harold St. John was only sixteen years old he attended a meeting where a blue-eyed, curly-headed baby of three wriggled frantically and slipped off her nurse's knee on to the floor. She was taken out; and young Harold chivalrously carried her home. Later on he liked to assert that he decided then and there to wait for that baby, but perhaps his memories were colored by subsequent events.

At any rate, there was always something rather special to him about little Ella Swain. Her rosy cheeks and healthy, normal appearance, her quick intelligence and tremendous enjoyment of life rested and refreshed him. She was no ascetic. Everything, from the nigger singing love songs on the beach, to the poems she learned at school, was delightful and golden. She lived to the full, and as his elder sister became her governess for a time he quite often saw her.

She was the daughter of Walter Rees Swain, H.M.I. and Alice Swain, and as her father was a Board of Education Inspector he naturally believed in a broad, careful education for girls. He was a scientist, and he delighted in introducing his small daughter to the wonders and beauties of the universe. There was an unusually close, tender link between Mr. Swain and his daughter, and Ella responded to his teaching with eager delight, and not only to science—history and poetry captivated her, and while her future husband experienced spiritual raptures in the meeting for the breaking of bread at Godalming, she would sit entranced, reciting Tennyson's poems to herself.

Her father's work meant frequent change of home, so Mr. Swain asked Mrs. St. John if she would take Ella as a weekly boarder, until she could start at Prior's Field, the new school which Mrs. Huxley (mother of Sir Julian and Aldous Huxley) was about to open near Godalming. She was then twelve years old, and her greatest delight was to play football in the square with their friends and the St. John boys. Harold, at twenty-four, loved to tease her and to pull her plait, and nicknamed her "Piglet." She remembers him as a very jolly young man, full of humour and high spirits, and occasionally she was allowed to go to an open air meeting and hold his hat, and this to her was the height of bliss. She lived with them for six months and then her family returned to Godalming. Later on she and Mrs. Swain came once more to stay with the St. Johns. And here it was that the rosy-faced sixteen year-old schoolgirl happened to attend some evening Bible Readings, intended primarily for young men, where Harold St. John lectured on the book of Amos.

These lectures opened her eyes. Up till then she had revered the Bible and deeply respected and believed her parents' teaching; but compared with botany and poetry, she found scripture a dull subject.

And as for St. Paul's missionary journeys and the kings of Israel, she considered them the depths of boredom! But through his exposition of the minor prophets, the Book suddenly became alive. Here in this deep, mystic, yet practical teaching was the bread her eager, growing spirit craved for—literary beauty and strength, scholarly truth, burning challenge and devotion. She responded from the depth of her soul, and night after night she would sit absorbed in the drawing-room with the young men, and whenever there was opportunity she would accompany Harold to the different halls where he lectured.

She was thrilled and fascinated and began to study her Bible, finding in it the answer to her youthful problems and a Book to live by. During the next two years Harold spent many Sundays lecturing down at Godalming, and he always stayed at her home; but although they were close friends, their relationship was quite devoid of romance. To her he was a revered teacher, twelve years her senior. And in all their intercourse they kept strictly to the point. He never failed to record these conversations in the diary.

"Traveled down in the train with Piglet. Much enjoyed Joshua 4 and 5 in the train together. An active, interested mind." "Wrote a long letter to P. on Matthew 13. A very dear child. God bless her and keep her in the midst of the vain glories of life." But in his heart there was growing a quiet, steady love, along with a fatherly interest in her spiritual growth. In September, 1906, he and another man interviewed her, with a view to her becoming a communicant.

"Saw P. as to the Lord's Table. A tender flower. Who will shelter her through life? God give him to be a true man. Never met anyone like her; God will give a great future." And a little later on, "A long think over future life. I feel drawn to P. if God's will. I think it would be truly happy."

He said nothing, for she, as yet, had no such ideas. She had gained an entry to read history at Westfield College, London University, and was as usual throwing herself into her plans and studies with heart and soul. He knew that this would mean a delay of at least three years; but with his constant selfless regard for her highest welfare, he did not attempt to dissuade her. He was now thirty-one and longing for a help meet and a home and children of his own.

"Great wave of homesickness and longing for a home of my own," he wrote. "Loneliness grows as I get spiritually separated from those around me. They don't understand me, nor I them. Thank God there will be children left here as long as I am. The heartstrings go out to them and I get awfully home sick—a man alone—a poor prospect. I long for a yoke fellow to be out and out for Christ."

So he waited patiently, while she enjoyed college life to the full. She became Senior Student, President of the Debating Society, and a loved friend of the Mistress and Founder of the College, Miss Constance L. Maynard, who dreamed a glorious academic career for her student. In her second year she won the Derby Scholarship for History, and later on was offered a Junior Lectureship at Holloway College, but she refused for family reasons. The future stretched bright before her, and then quite suddenly Harold St. John proposed to her, crossing the road at Brighton, in the middle of the heavy traffic. It was a complete surprise to her, but, because for years he had been "the best and most saintly man I knew," she accepted immediately, and they announced their engagement that night at the supper table.

She had expected to become a housewife in Bayswater, with a banker husband already rising to prosperity, but this idea, too, had to be abandoned. Some months later Harold St. John astonished all who knew him by deciding to resign from the Bank and to go abroad as a foreign missionary without any settled means of support. This was no sudden impulse: years before he had seen the vision, but the time was not yet ripe. It had seemed impracticable then for family reasons and he had resigned himself rather sadly to London life. The land that had previously filled his thoughts was Mexico, where his own father had died.

"Mexico looms before me," he had written about five years previously. "'Go ye,' Christ said, and I can do it in the Name. Mexico took Papa; can I carry her the gospel? Perhaps a second purpose lurks behind, to preach Him where He is not named, but what of Mother?" "It is easy to put Mexico away and settle in ease and comfort, but I am hungry to find myself without a plank between me and Christ. Is Mexico God's will? I dare not move until I am clearer about my motives." And then later on, "Mexico must go. I must settle down to a

London life. A bitter, bitter prospect, only sweetened by 'His wisdom ever waketh.'"

But the seed of desire had lain latent through the years and at thirty-six he was free to go—not to Mexico, but to South America. The sudden knowledge came to him in the night, and he came down in the morning, absolutely certain of his call. The only words he could find to explain this revelation were the words of the hymn,

Christ, the Son of God, hath sent me
To the midnight lands;
Mine the mighty ordination,
Of the pierced hands.

To the sorrow and indignation of his employers, he resigned his excellent prospects and proceeded to prepare himself for the mission field. "He would have undoubtedly risen to the top," said his colleagues regretfully, and the deputy manager was frankly sceptical.

"How will you live, and who will provide for your expenses," he asked, "since you are not going out under any recognized missionary society?" "I'm going out to do God's work," replied Harold. "God is sending me, and God will provide." "Well, St. John," replied the manager thoughtfully, "I wish I had your faith."

He spent a year in the missionary training home in North West Hampstead, and did a course in Homeopathic Medicine and First Aid. And here at the college he was remembered by one who only knew him for a few months and who later was ordained. About forty-five years later he wrote:

"In the year 1912 six of us entered the missionary training home in North West Hampstead, to prepare ourselves for God's work. We were all bound for different places. Mr. St. John and I shared the same table and the same study and the same classroom and we loved each other's company. He usually carried his umbrella, and often we climbed Hampstead Heath to enjoy, like the two who went to Emmaus, the enlightening presence of the Third who drew near and went with us. He was so humble and so devoted to his studies. He used to admire our knowledge of the Scriptures, but we knew that this was his own humility. He was destined for greatness. He followed One Who humbled Himself and was exalted."

Ella Swain, meanwhile, was doing a special missionary nursing course at the Mildmay Hospital. She and Harold were now in London together, and although the off-duty hours of a nurse in those days were few and short, he did manage to take her out once a fortnight. Miss Cattell, the saintly old matron of the Mildmay, disapproved of this. She considered it almost fast behavior and suggested to Ella that another nurse should go with them and act as chaperone. Ella, who loved the old matron dearly, hesitated, and in order to gain time, said she would discuss it with her fiancé. She did, but he cut the discussion short. "Tell old muscatels and raisins I'm not having any," he replied, and they set off on their indecorous expedition to the country.

From Bethnal Green Ella went to Brighton where she did her midwifery and worked on the district. They were married in July, 1914, and a special reception had to be given for proud mothers and babies after the wedding. The wedding service was conducted by Mr. James Hamilton, the beloved leader from Clarendon Room, Notting Hill, whom Harold regarded as a spiritual father. Thus, after twelve years of patient waiting, Harold was given his heart's desire—the wife who, in every way, was the perfect complement of himself. Together they decided quite simply that throughout their married life the Lord's work would always come first with him, and she never forgot her promise or questioned his long absences from home. Her practicality balanced his mysticism, for she was a born home-maker; and whether in the wilds of Brazil, or in their verminous lodgings in Buenos Aires, or later in England, where the old red brick house swarmed with children, there was always a place of peace for him to return to, where he could rest from the heavy strain of the ministry and study undisturbed. She asked very little of him, for she was essentially a giver, and for over forty years the calm, deep, selfless quality of their love for each other impressed even casual visitors. No child of theirs can ever remember one sharp, irritable word between them, and the atmosphere of the home inspired many young people to whom they opened it so freely.

"I want my home to be exactly like yours," wrote one young bride. And when at last the earthly parting came many were the testimonies to the influence of that home.

"I thank God for the wonderful example your united lives have been," wrote a well-known missionary from India, "and for the privilege I had of being drawn into your family circle and experiencing the happy atmosphere of love and harmony that seemed to permeate the very walls of your home."

"The love you had for each other was such a powerful witness and example to anyone who saw and watched you," wrote a school teacher who had stayed with them as a child. And from another who had known them closely all through her childhood, "I always thought you were a model of what a husband and wife should be—so much one in everything, and always so radiantly happy together. I am convinced that it was a sermon to the young people who watched you."

There were letters, too, from some who had never been blessed with a happy home life. They watched wistfully, almost wondering if such a relationship could be true.

"You can't possibly know how much your life together has meant to me," wrote one. "It meant, perhaps, more than the preaching and teaching, though I've never heard anyone to compare with him. But you knew that if you came for advice, you would always receive a welcome. There would always be a readiness to listen and to turn your problems into prayer. And you would go away thinking, 'It's going to be all right now.'"

"My heart goes out in praise for all the blessing your wonderful love to each other has been to me and scores of others," added another. "I remember about thirteen years ago the first tremendous impression it made upon me, and how it made me feel that if that was what the love of Christ manifested in human relationships was like, then there was indeed no love like His."

Another faithful old servant of Christ wrote: "My mind goes back to an evening I spent in your home at Malvern, twenty years ago. Commander and Mrs. Salway and Douglas Brealey were also there. There was such a happy atmosphere that I have frequently said it was the nearest thing to heaven I have ever experienced."

But this was all far ahead. Their first home was one room in a house in Buenos Aires where black beetles swarmed the walls at night and they stood the legs of their camp beds in kerosene, and Ella learned to

MR. AND MRS. HAROLD ST. JOHN

housekeep in a kitchen which they shared with four Spanish families. It was a hard struggle from the beginning, but fortunately both were endowed with a keen sense of humour, and Ella was his sunshine and laughter. "She's like a humming-bird chained to a tortoise," he once remarked. One feature of their life together was that he was never in the least particular as to what he called her. She answered indiscriminately to Tinker, Claud, Keren-Happuch, or Jemima, Jones, or William.

In his old age, when quiet sanity and balance were some of his most distinguishing marks, he was reading a pamphlet on the crucified life. "A crucified Christian can live independent of country, wife or child. He is at home in any clime, and has yielded up all preferences," ran the pamphlet. He stopped, considered a moment, and then declared his disagreement with the statement, and, using one of his pet names for his wife, he said, "I think I would still rather have Ahithophel!"

CHAPTER 5

The Missionary

THE view of the face of the Man gets clearer. Oh, my I adorable Lord," wrote Harold St. John in 1909. But there had been times of deep depression and introspection, and when he left the Bank in 1913 and offered himself as a foreign missionary, he sought a new equipment for a new task and received, so his oldest living friend, Mr. Wanhill, tells us, a mighty filling of the Holy Spirit. As far as is known, he himself only ever once spoke openly of this experience. And when asked in later life what views he held on the doctrine of the second blessing he was reticent and non-committal, maintaining that a measured supply of grace was given according to the need or magnitude of the task, save in the case of Christ Himself, of Whom it is said, "God giveth not the Spirit by measure unto Him." Yet there is no doubt that at this time he underwent some experience too sacred to speak about, that lifted him into a radiance and freedom that he had never known before. The rather solemn, self-conscious holiness gave way to a sort of uncalculating joy, as though he no longer had to watch his step in the heavenlies; he was at home there, self-forgetful, absorbed in Christ.

Nearly forty-four years later, when he lay on his death-bed, he called his daughter who was sitting close beside him, in the middle of the night. His face was alight with the joy of an old, loved memory, his voice was urgent though his breath was failing. "Did you ever see God?" he whispered. "No, Daddy," she answered. "I did," came the labored reply, "long, long ago. I've never told anyone about it, but I'll tell you now, when I've had a little rest."

His eyes closed and he sank into unconsciousness. The details of the secret of that long life were never revealed, but the truth of the secret was evident. As F. W. H. Myers wrote of the man who has seen God:

Who that one moment has the least descried Him,
   Dimly and faintly, hidden and afar,
Doth not despise all excellence beside Him,
   Pleasures and powers that are not, or that are?

Yea, amid all men bear himself thereafter,
   Smit with a solemn and a sweet surprise,
Dumb to their scorn, and turning on their laughter
   Only the dominance of earnest eyes.

Harold St. John was recommended by the brethren in his local assembly, and a meeting was held for prayer and the laying on of hands. He took great pains to discover about the history and religion of South America, as one of his farewell addresses given in Sheffield and London in 1914 shows. These addresses, full of eloquence and fervor, kindled many of his younger hearers.

"The chief business of every Christian in the world today is to evangelize. No consideration of age or sex, poverty or rank, allows you to escape. May I say that your first thought is not your wife, nor your baby, nor yet your business; these are side issues only. The one controlling thing that lies before you is that your business in the world is to preach the gospel to every creature. Again I say, your life's business in the world is to preach the gospel to every creature, if you bear the name of Christian at all. When you meet Jesus face to face, the first thing He will ask you will not be, 'How did you conduct your business in the world?' but 'How did you preach My gospel? How did you care for My interests? Were you a witness to Me? Were you one who bore the standard high, and carried the light of My gospel clear and shining through this world?' Oh, see to it that you are not one of whom He shall need to be ashamed. It is the responsibility of the Church of God to wipe out the stain that rests upon her, that half the world has as yet heard nothing of Christ, and yet it's nearly nineteen hundred years since our Lord stood in Galilee and said, 'Go ye into all the world and preach the gospel to every creature.' Perhaps before we come back some of the young men here may have been led of God to go to South America to preach the gospel. We shall have nothing but the plain story of the Cross of

Christ, of His resurrection and His return. These truths constitute our stock in trade, the goods that the Lord Jesus is sending us to trade with in those distant parts.

"We are being led forth in peace. You can have this world's peace and enjoy it provided you shut your eyes to the future and shut the gates of the soul to yesterday. The peace that the Lord Jesus gives is precisely the opposite: it throws back the gates of yesterday showing sins forgiven, and as to tomorrow, it opens its gates and shows the future, radiant with hope and with the certainty of seeing His face.

"The Lord's way of sending out His disciples is the best way today (Luke 10:2-4). If we are spared to come back here, He may ask us as He asked those laborers, 'When I sent you without purse and shoes and scrip, lacked ye anything?' The temporal needs of His servants are known to the Lord Jesus, and their spiritual needs are considerably more important than their temporal needs."

It was not an easy time to set out on missionary work, with other young men enlisting on every hand; but although he weighed up the relative claims of patriotism carefully, the call to go forward was too clear to be set aside, and they set off from Tilbury Docks on the 29th of October, 1914, in the *Highland Rover*. It must have been a moving parting, for the seas were infested with submarines, and the sister ship, the *Highland Hope,* had been sunk some weeks previously. As the ship moved away from the dock, Harold leaned over the rail and called out to his mother, "Remember, let not your heart be troubled."

They had need of courage. The friend who was to have met them in Buenos Aires had been called away on military service, and they arrived in this strange land unmet and with no knowledge of the language. However, he had an address in the poorer quarter of the town, which they found after some difficulty, and when at length they arrived and darkness fell, the cockroaches emerged from their hiding places and climbed up the walls in hundreds. The little kitchen and wash room had to be shared with four native families, so getting a meal was not as easy as it sounds. If Ella's heart sank, she did not show it. She merely stood the legs of the beds in tins of kerosene and began to clean. Harry was genuinely delighted and wrote joyfully of "the mercy of God in finding us such a suitable home." They had brought all necessary furniture with them—two camp beds, one folding table, chair and washstand.

In many ways it *was* wonderfully suitable, as through such close intercourse with the Spanish families they picked up the language remarkably quickly. In spite of their lonely start they soon got to know the Christians at the Mission Evangélique and were warmly welcomed at the meetings. Before three months were up, Harold wrote:

"We are very happy and working as hard as the extreme heat will allow. Spanish, Scripture, housework, etc., keep us quite busy every day, and I have given away a few hundred tracts in some of the big squares. But of course I cannot attempt to speak to the people yet. I cannot write much as I have nothing to say of any great spiritual interest; one's own soul's story can never be written on paper, but it's a time of thinking and praying and weighing the possible future."

At the New Year, Dr. and Mrs. Lowe kindly fixed them up in a little bungalow adjoining a meeting room in a suburb. Both were making rapid progress in the language, and in the spring Harold was invited to go on a preaching tour into Bolivia with Mr. Payne, a veteran pioneer missionary of the Argentine. Meanwhile, Ella went to look after a missionary who was expecting her second baby.

Thrilled with the prospect of work at last, Harold set out to join his leader, traveling, by choice, in a sort of cattle truck, designed to hold the very poorest travelers. He employed the journey for distributing tracts to his sixty fellow passengers and holding conversations over the plentiful supplies of food and wine without which no Spaniard ever travels. Arriving at Catamarca on the Friday morning he was met by Mr. Payne and Mr. Stacey. Harold must have been tired after thirty-eight hours in the truck, but he seems to have plunged straight into a great gospel campaign. Huge open air meetings were held each afternoon in the Square for ten days, and a large hall was crowded every night.

From Catamarca Mr. Payne and Harold rode off into the high forests and mists of the Sierra mountains to visit a lonely Christian family, following the river tracks till they reached a pass. They finished their journey in the dark, along a dubious road crossed by unbridged streams, till they reached the little ranch with its mud hut and tin shed. After fourteen hours in the saddle they were thankful for the warm welcome of those isolated Christians. For three years they had kept a little guest room ready for some servant of the Lord, but this was the first time anyone had visited them.

The guest room had also been used for a menagerie of animals, and the two visitors slept soundly in company with the dog, several hens, goats and a parrot. For three days they stayed, holding meetings, visiting, teaching; and one man who had been a persecutor for years confessed Christ. Harold also treated a number of sick people, and before they left, the little group gathered in the tin hut for a communion service. Up in this primitive country hamlet he was able to preach for the first time in Spanish, and his cup of joy was full.

After six weeks of this sort of life he rejoined Ella in Cordova and they set up home again in two rented rooms, studying, and visiting with Mr. Payne lonely groups of Christians up in the mountains, distributing tracts, preaching and teaching. Harold was again being drawn back to that line of work to which God had called him in England, not primarily the work of an evangelist, but the feeding of the flock of God. In May, 1915, he wrote:

"I have thought much of the glory of the pastor's gift. 'He gave some, apostles, prophets, evangelists, pastors and teachers.' The Giver of all these gifts exercised each one Himself. He was an Apostle (Hebrews 3:1), a Prophet (Acts 3:22), an Evangelist (Luke 4:18), a Teacher (John 3:2); but He never says, 'I am the good Apostle, Prophet, etc.' He only says, 'I am the good Pastor, the good Pastor giveth His life for the sheep.' This would appear to be in contrast with old time pastors; with them the sheep died for the shepherd Abel took a first-born of his sheep. With Christ, the Shepherd dies for the flock. For many it is of vastly more value to care for souls, to visit and spend one's strength for the flock and its needs, than it is to preach to audiences gathered to a regular meeting. Both are needed, but the permanent work of a devoted pastor is beyond calculation. Would not every gathering of Christians in England be in a good state, growing in love and knowledge, with increasing numbers and success in the gospel, if one of its number would yield himself to the Lord with the avowed purpose of laying down his life for the sake of the flock, simply because the sheep are His? No official seal is needed, no human approval is required. Love for Christ, linked with love for the sheep, is sufficient equipment."

This last work of visiting lonely Christians took him far afield, at times as far as the borders of Paraguay, and once he writes of their visiting small groups of believers in the bare forest lands of the Chaco, riding from point to point and finding great interest.

"The work in this part is simply due to the reading of God's Word. Bibles got into the hands of two or three women in one village and a couple of woodcutters in another. They obeyed the truth, and now with very little human help they meet together to read the Scriptures. We found them full of questions, and, as it is their habit to jot down any difficulties, when a visitor comes a list is produced which may take hours to answer. The life here is rough and hard. I calculated that for ten consecutive days our bed allowance averaged three and three-quarter hours a night. There was little temptation to sloth, as lying with one side roasting at a smoky charcoal fire and the other freezing is not conducive to dreams, especially if you wake with your neighbor's feet in your face. I smuggled a piece of soap and a toothbrush in with the Gospels, but I find little opportunity and no encouragement to use either. Water is scarce, washing and bathing are regarded as English eccentricities. But it is surprising how contentedly one turns out at 5:00 a.m., unwashed and unbreakfasted."

Sitting in mud huts, opening up the treasures of the Bible to the very poor, distributing Gospels in the prison, visiting a woman dying of consumption until she accepted Christ and went joyfully Home to Him, and preaching in the open air, kept Harold busy all day and most evenings. He was often away from home and for a time lodged with a barber and his family and a lot of other people in a little square room with a soft brick floor, so he could not put his socks on the ground for an instant without their turning red. The only furniture was a bed and chair. He washed in the public yard, with an appreciative audience. His room had a door but no window or air outlet but a tiny grating; but he managed all right, although the heat was suffocating. In spite of the heat and the hardship he was radiantly happy, living to the full and using every opportunity.

Ella, left behind in the home in Cordova with her Argentinian neighbors, was progressing well with Spanish and was already beginning to take part in women's meetings, but her first baby was on the way and she was feeling very unwell. However, mercifully there were English missionaries within easy reach, and to this day she remembers with deep gratitude the kindness and friendship of the Paynes and Mr. Gilbert Lear. When Harry came home he always found her bright and uncomplaining although very thin, but surely it was in the providence of God that just at that point news reached her of her father's serious illness, and she and her husband agreed that it would be better for her to return home, as he was not expected to live. He died two weeks after her arrival, and she remained with her mother, resting and cared for, until, three months later, on January 2nd, 1916, a daughter was born, and the mother wrote:

"A great joy has come to us with the New Year. On January 2nd God sent Harry and me a little girl to comfort us all. She is at this moment sleeping very cosily in her pink and white cot beside me and is so dear; very strong, with a shock of dark hair and big blue yes. Her name is Hazel Margaret."

So the lonely man, riding his horse over the Sierra Mountains, reached Cordova one night to be greeted by a cable announcing the birth of his daughter. "I take the tidings as one more addition to the countless mercies with which my singularly happy life has been strewn," he wrote; and with his usual thoroughness he acquired a large teddy bear and a book of Nursery Rhymes which he studied and memorized along with his Greek lexicons and Spanish commentaries.

CHAPTER 6

The Shepherd

ELLA was delayed in England longer than expected owing to an operation for appendicitis and the impossibility of getting a passage back in war time. And Harry scoured the wild countryside on horseback, on extraordinarily fruitful missionary journeys with Mr. Payne in Bolivia and Paraguay. He tells of a man who stood up in the middle of a meeting and asked to be allowed to confess Christ; of another who traveled thirty miles to be saved; of a young woman, twenty-seven years of age, with consumption, who died clearly resting in the finished work of Christ. He must have traveled hundreds of miles, too, over the Argentinian Mountains, seeking out lonely isolated Christians. "At each little hut we dismount," he wrote, "give them any news we have, gather as many as we can, and then the Book is produced, a few verses read, and very simply and tenderly we show them God's way of peace. Prayer is offered and a hymn sung, and we remount and pass on our way. One morning we had to see a quarry man, a few miles away, who begins work at 6:00 a.m. so our start had to be early. We found that the rough life of a mining camp had dimmed the brightness of his joy in Christ, and we had a quiet, solemn time, leaving him to the care of the One who taught David to say, 'He restoreth my soul.'"

From April to June Harold accompanied Mr. Strange in his motor launch, visiting the islands of the River Plate. It was bitterly cold and in Harold's words, "The people are as simple as they are dirty. One man remarked in self-defence, when I commented on his condition, 'Well, I washed last October!' Another said, 'As for me, I wouldn't bathe for twenty dollars.' We were able to hold meetings in two houses, and in one case all the audience came by boat, some thirty people having braved distance, darkness, the bitter cold and the hidden dangers of the river, to hear the gospel preached.

"One of the Christians we met was a certain Don Enrika; he had been a publican with a good business, but when the grace of God conquered him he gave up his calling and when I met him he was earning a very few shillings a week, working in winter up to his knees in mud, cutting down rushes for basket makers. As may be supposed, he and his large family were radiantly happy in their deep poverty. Christ has many shining jewels in this land, who shame me with their self denial and their realization of the demand and the appeal of the Cross as motives for self-consecration. With them, an elementary sense of justice will not allow them to offer less than all to the Son of God."

During July Harold was off again on a walking tour through Uruguay. During that journey he traveled the rough country roads on foot for a distance of 350 kilometers, sleeping on mud and brick floors. He tells of an increasing exhilaration in preaching the Cross, and also of the loving kindness and care of his God every step of the way. Two incidents stand out clearly.

"Late one evening my companion and I were finishing a long day's march, laden with a stock of books. For some miles we had followed a mere track across the hills, and at length with gathering dusk we could no longer see the way. It was mid-winter and bitterly cold, and we were several miles from the village. My companion was a good deal less hardy than myself, and to sleep out of doors would be unthinkable. It was too wet to make a fire. I prayed that God would find us a way, not suggesting how He should do it, but remembering Gerhardt Tersteegen's excellent remark, 'I am my Father's child, but not His privy councillor.' Even as I was praying we heard the sound of wheels, and out of the gloom appeared a rough sort of coach whose driver hailed us and offered to carry us to the village. It appeared that a rich farmer had suddenly become ill and a doctor had been called, and the coach which had conveyed him was now on its return journey.

"A second incident was a gentler touch of God's hand. When I had come down from the north to meet my wife it was hot weather, and I only had my lightest clothes on. Owing to the impossibility of her getting a passage, several months elapsed before her arrival, and I found myself traveling in an icy winter with very little protection from the cold. My boxes were stored, the price of new clothes was exorbitant;

so I laid the matter before God and waited. Two days later at the close
of a meeting a Christian tailor came to me and said, 'I have a suit left
on my hands by a defaulting customer. I fancy it might fit you, but it
may be too small, or you may not like the material.' I replied that if the
Lord intended it for me He would certainly choose good material and
as to my size, even the very hairs of my head were all numbered, so my
friend need be under no apprehension. As might be expected, I found
myself two days later well and warmly clothed."

Meanwhile Ella and Hazel had set sail through the dangerous seas
of 1916. It was not a pleasant crossing as conditions were definitely
war-time, and large black rats who nibbled the mother's toes at night
made her afraid to sleep lest her baby be bitten. Little Hazel became
ill as they passed into the tropics, nor was the atmosphere of the cabin
in the first place improved by the very strong cheese which their Por-
tuguese traveling companion kept under her bed. Perhaps, however,
it deflected the rats from the baby's toes! But conditions improved as
they neared the Equator, and on the 27th they sighted Montevideo.
Husband and wife caught sight of each other far away, she holding up
Hazel in a blue pelisse, and he holding up the large teddy-bear.

The pleasant three-roomed cottage, as Harold described the little
home he had rented, where Ella remained working among the neigh-
boring women during his frequent absences, was soon no longer quite
so pleasant owing to a bad break down in the water and drainage systems during an extra ordinarily hot spell of weather. Hazel was really
ill, and they moved up to Los Cocos, high in the hills. Here, as Harold
wrote, "Life was simple, but quite civilized, though only two nights
ago a stampede of animals swept past, and I was told in the morning
that wild beasts had passed looking for prey and had found two sheep."
It was a beautiful place, greatly enriched by the friendship and loving
kindness of the Blairs and the Sugdens, and the little home looked
down a valley forty miles long, studded with villages. Harold's heart
was burdened for this valley. In April, 1917, he wrote, "I wondered
whether the Lord might call me to help His servants to evangelize this
quiet valley. Many of the people have heard the gospel, and probably
every home has received Christian literature."

Although Harold's heart yearned over the needs of the valley, he
was still most drawn to the Christians with their pitiful lack of pastoral

care and teaching. And when early in 1917 Mr. Stuart McNair, a warrior pioneer missionary, came from Brazil and discussed the possibility of a Bible School, Harold was intensely interested. In February, 1917, he set off; first by boat, and then on foot, to look into the matter more closely.

Mr. McNair had worked for twenty years in Brazil in a sparsely populated district, and owing to his devoted labor believers gathered from many miles round on Sunday morning, sometimes traveling a day's journey over the hills. The two missionaries visited every little Christian gathering within a radius of fifty miles, often preaching many times a day, and of these comparatively ignorant believers Harold writes, "Summarizing my impressions of the meetings, what pleased me most was that brethren seemed to have learned largely from Scripture itself and comparatively little from human ministry. This gives a tone of great freshness and simplicity. Most of us who, like myself, have seen modern missionary work abroad, have been struck by the essentially English character of the teaching and church organization, second hand discipline being much to the fore." But they were hungry and thirsty for teaching, and Harold had caught the vision. He hurried back to the Argentine just in time for the birth of his first son. But as soon as the mother and child were strong enough they packed up and started off on the 3,500 kilometer journey to Carangola from Los Cocos. Farnham was seven weeks old, and even the optimistic Harold described it as "the most difficult journey" he'd ever undertaken. It was very rough, and the boat was extremely crowded. Wherever they stayed they were plagued by insects. They took all their worldly possessions with them, which caused the official in charge of the customs to remark, "Times have changed since the days of the early apostles who went out without purse or scrip!" Harold replied humbly enough that the apostles did not have to travel with babies, and sought to turn the conversation to higher channels.

But even the last ten miles, riding on mules over rough tracks in the dark, came to an end at last, and they were installed on the top floor of Mr. McNair's house. By September the two missionaries were sending out leaflets to all the scattered groups of Christians, informing them of the new Bible School in Carangola. The leaflet ran thus:

BIBLE SCHOOL IN CARANGOLA

In the early days of November we propose to begin a Bible School with a view to helping young men who wish to grow up in the knowledge of the Scriptures, and also to perfect themselves in grammar and other studies.

The classes will continue for six months, the lessons occupying from 5:00 to 8:00 p.m., thus leaving the day free for students to earn their living.

The students will not be involved in any expense beyond the purchase of lesson books, but we cannot accept responsibility as to their maintenance. Each must manage his manner of life and work with his neighbors.

Any applicant who is unknown to us must produce letters of commendation signed by persons in whom we have confidence.

Our chief desire is that there may be an atmosphere of prayer and spiritual power, in order that, while progressing in study, there may be still more progress in the knowledge of God.

STUART MCNAIR
HAROLD ST. JOHN.

Twelve students had booked by November, almost all working in the coffee or sugar fields from dawn till late afternoon. A number of local visitors would also drift in to the evening sessions, so the little room was often quite full. Reading, geography, elementary mathematics, were taught by Mr. McNair. Harold took the Bible Classes. He chose the Tabernacle and Romans as his opening theme, and a weekly examination was given; and at the weekends the students scattered far and wide to preach the gospel. During the day Harold did medical work, as to bring a doctor from the nearest city would have cost upwards of five pounds. Leprosy was not uncommon and practically no precautions were taken as to contagion. He speaks of lepers freely partaking of the communion cup in the country meetings, and he tells of a man with terrible ulcers on his leg whom he visited constantly for seven weeks and who was finally converted. This man's mother believed, too, and the house became a local dispensary and meeting room.

The Bible School in Carangola was a sort of pioneer venture. Its spiritual results quickly proved to be deep and worth while. The Spirit worked freely in the hearts of that group of simple, single-minded young lads, and many went forth from the Bible School as able ministers and evangelists.

There were certain sound principles on which the School was based, one being the understanding that there was from the beginning that it was an indigenous effort. The young men supported themselves as far as possible but any unavoidable deficit was made up by the local Christians. There was no question of these boys being favoured by the missionaries, for the local church and the lads in training were a unit. The lectures were free and open to all. Local Christians who had no opportunity of entering the ministry were welcome to share the teaching, and they all felt a responsibility for the future evangelists. Of this situation Harold wrote at the beginning of their third year:

"In respect of food, we are giving more variety and spending some hundreds of dollars more than in the last school, but we found that local brethren refused to let us shoulder any extra expense, so the difference was more than made up by collections and local gifts. Brethren have understood the laws of Christian giving very well, many faithfully dedicating a tithe of all land produce to the Lord's work, so we are able to build meeting rooms and assist Brazilian workers without any outside appeal being made. Such men naturally prosper, spiritually and materially."

There was no educational barrier; reading and writing were taught as well as Greek and English. They asked for three qualifications only in their students—love for Christ, a desire to learn, a yearning to win souls. So it is no surprise to read in one of Harold's letters, "A nice black who can hardly read has just arrived to join the School. He's walked over twenty-three miles, carrying his box over awful rivers. He looks exactly as though he had just stepped off Southend Beach with a set of bones to clap and he is irresistibly funny."

Like Mr. McNair, he was to these boys, teacher, friend and father.

"I am doing my best," he wrote to his wife in 1920, after she had stayed at home with the children, "to give myself more than ever before to the students; I mean, by personal intercourse. They come to me at all hours to consult, and this morning I had six in on all kinds of private difficulties. It is very nice for me to be mixing up with these simple, true young fellows. The morning reading is what I enjoy most, when we have a hymn or two and then get to work. It's always a great crush. This morning I spoke a good deal on marriage and the ideal we ought to have for our women. Isn't this a poky letter? But all the time I'm trying to talk to you, folk will talk to me, and ulcerous legs keep coming up for treatment."

Every aspect of their lives, spiritual, mental and domestic, was included in the thorough, careful teaching these boys received. Then Miss McNair, who joined her brother in 1919, started classes on baby care for Christian wives, which Harold apparently attended, for he writes of them in detail.

"The lectures are good and practical about feeding babies, cleanliness, etc.—just what we need, and the women swarm in. Leonore's baby began to weep bitterly in the middle and she banged it on the back, and it only wept louder. So I took it from her, rubbed its wee back, put its five week's old head on my shoulder, and it went sound asleep, much to Leonore's amusement. You would have loved to have seen all the sisters. Poor Doña Raymondo, sitting listening! I wonder if she was thinking of those six tiny graves up the hill, and who can say by whose fault they are there?"

The lads were growing in grace; the local Christians had offered to build a house ready for his wife and family to return to him, and Harold was supremely happy in his work. "I am utterly in my element and as happy as a king, except for you and the babies," he wrote. And on another occasion,

"Perhaps it is your prayers that are making these days so bright and peaceful. I wake each morning with a peculiar sense of joy in God, and find all the work goes with a lift and a lilt. We had a very serious time this morning, on building character of stone or brick. I was showing in Genesis 11:3, Isaiah 9:10 and 65:3 how brick is man's little temporary makeshift to avoid a crisis, but God uses stones, and living ones, too, for His work. The boys were keenly interested, and the time of prayer after was very earnest. Things are certainly moving. For any man to live in a healthy climate, in a district where everyone is good to him, with work that admits no idle moment and yet utterly satisfies without a shadow of anxiety, and to crown all, the knowledge of the peace of God, is certainly to be without anything more to ask of life."

And yet he did ask more. There seemed everything to hold him. The love of the local Christians and the students, the friendship of the

McNairs, the invaluable work he was doing and, most of all, the prospect of his family's return. But the Bible School was established and prospering and would continue to prosper under Mr. McNair's able guidance; and there were other districts, and other countries, where no such effort had been made, and the young Christians were hungry and thirsty for teaching. Already letters were reaching him to come and hold Bible Schools in British Guiana, the West Indies, the States.

Everywhere he went he was smitten by the eager thirst of Christians for able, Spirit-filled teaching. He tells of a visit to a large, happy family in a log hut, all converted, who immediately went to get their neighbors to a meeting. It was 6:00 p.m. and he had not dined, so he hinted that the Scriptural rule was first that which is carnal and next that which is spiritual. But the crowd was already arriving, so at 6:30 the meeting started, and lasted till 9:15. Just as they finished, another lot of neighbors arrived from a distance, so another meeting was held, lasting till 11:15 p.m. Then dinner was produced and at midnight Harold lay down on the boards to sleep, but at 4:30 a.m. he was wakened by his host, who stuck his head through the window and called out, "Dear brother, can you give me any light on the 9th chapter of the book of Revelation?" "So," adds Harold, "we entertained each other with the things of God till it was time for the train. And I wonder how many of my readers would be as vigorous and bright as these folk if they had a visit from a like-minded Christian perhaps once a year."

The final decision must have cost him much. It meant up-rooting himself from that first, dear Bible School, but, much more, it meant embarking on a life of constant travel in which his wife and three babies could no longer join him. It was the choice between the home of his own, that had been offered him at Carangola, and separation. His wife yearned to come back to Carangola, but never once did she attempt to influence his decision. That was made before God alone, and in 1921 he left Brazil for the last time and traveled up to British Guiana to gather together the Christians for a season of teaching.

It was to be his life's work till the end: constant travel, ceaseless activity; and in many parts of the world Christian men and women have been kindled and led into blessing through his ministry and his exposition of the Word of God. It was hard, self-denying work, but he was radiantly happy in it from beginning to end; indeed, he never envisaged any end. Early in his Christian life he had written joyfully in the old diary, "When I go Home, work will begin in eternity the very next morning. Life is not a blind alley; it's a thoroughfare, closing in twilight, opening in dawn."

CHAPTER 7

Father of Five

THE Lord loveth the gates of Zion, more than all the dwellings of Jacob.' What does that mean? It means that while He loves your home—(don't make any mistake about that, He loves your house, and wants you to devote it to God)—there is one thing He loves more, and that is His Own house and His interests on earth. So remember, that in your thinking you always give the first place to the house of God, and the next to your own house. The Lord loves the gates of Zion more than all the dwellings of Jacob. The assembly of Christians is God's chief interest in this world, so let it be yours; and if you take care of God's house, He will take care of yours. But if you make your house the first concern you will find that He will leave you to your own business." (Part of a sermon given by Mr. St. John on Psalm 87.)

The decision to leave the upbringing of his children mainly to his wife was not taken lightly. Nor would it have been taken at all had he not had complete, almost blind, confidence in her wisdom and ability. They had agreed at their marriage that family ties should never hinder his work for God and neither ever looked back on that decision. Yet he had always loved children and was, innately, a father. From the moment when he purchased the book of Nursery Rhymes and solemnly memorized "Humpty Dumpty" and its like, jogging on horseback through the forests, to the last week of his life when with laboring breath and wandering memory he still gathered his failing senses and prayed for his five by name, his children were never really out of his thoughts, although there are few men who can have seen less of them in their childhood. As has already been pointed out, his first baby was eight months old before he saw her. But the next two and a half years he was intimately concerned with the little son whom they so nearly lost. Farnham was only three weeks old when his father left home early one morning to conduct a wedding in Buenos Aires, nearly sixty miles

HAROLD ST. JOHN WITH HIS SONS AND DAUGHTERS
Left to right: HAZEL (Margaret); FARNHAM (Allen Rees); JOHN (Michael Spenser); OLIVER (Beauchamp); PATRICIA (Mary)

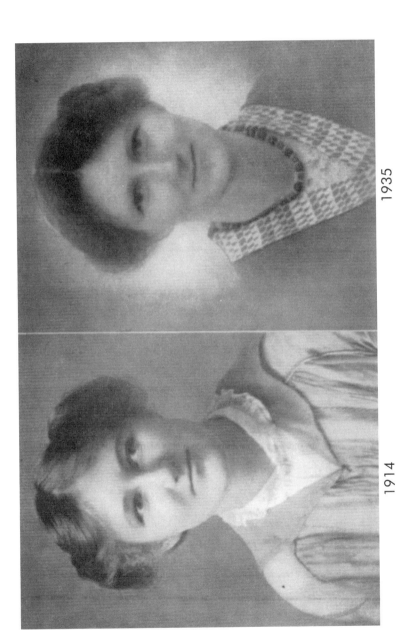

1914

1935

MRS. HAROLD ST. JOHN

away, promising to return the following night. But at the close of the meeting Harold discovered that the train had been canceled; indeed there was no hope of a train for another four days to the remote country district where he lived. The missionaries were delighted to offer him accommodation, but they did not know Harold St. John. Drawn by the thought of that little new son he set out to walk over the mountain ranges. All night he walked and all the next day. Very late the following evening he reached home at the time appointed, footsore and weary, but delighted to be back, and indulging, no doubt, in his bad habit of stealing up to the cot where Hazel lay and waking her up to entertain him for half an hour or so over his supper, after which he would pace endlessly up and down the room, crooning Moody and Sankey hymns in his efforts to get the thoroughly roused, chuckling baby to sleep again.

In 1918 the family evacuated their quarters in the Bible School in order to make room for more students on the premises, and moved into what Ella dubbed, "The House of the Thousand Fleas." Pigs had lived under the floor with the last owner, and the rats visited them freely; nor was it a particularly peaceful spot for the young mother.

"I prefer not to be away at night unless absolutely necessary," wrote her husband. "Ella's appearance strikes the popular imagination, as it has mine for years. They credit her with fabulous wealth. On three successive nights uninvited persons have tried to get into the house." Nevertheless it was roomy and airy, and perhaps no little home has ever been more beloved by its owners or held dearer memories; for although the family limited his travels, it was an inestimable help in gaining the confidence of the neighbors. The coming of this friendly young mother into their midst was a never-ending source of interest and delight to the native sisters, as were also her few simple belongings, and Ella unconsciously solved the problem of suitable headgear for the morning meeting by sending out her washing to an old negress. She was mildly surprised one Sunday morning to recognize a couple of her face towels adorning the heads of the congregation. However, as the articles were all returned later in the week in a clean condition, no questions were asked and the custom persisted.

They were a loving, simple, truly Christian congregation, and they loved their new missionaries who so quickly learned to live and speak as they did. Harold wrote of them, "They use the Lord's Name on every occasion, with great reverence, and one was not surprised to hear a voice recently from the kitchen, 'Here is some maize left over from dinner, Cecilia; if God so pleases you must fry it tomorrow.' 'Surely, if it is the Lord's will.' But I was, I confess, hardly satisfied when, on asking a young woman for her address, she replied, 'The Lord Jesus knows it.' True, but for me it hardly helped matters!"

Little "Pakita," as they called Hazel, played barefoot with her Brazilian friends and spoke their language and became almost as brown as they were. But baby "Nana" did not thrive. He became ill with a lingering dysentery, complicated by abscesses in his ears. He lay very quiet in his cot, too weak to move, except to raise one skinny arm to his mother's face and blow small, pitiful kisses. Careful feeding and nursing seemed of no avail and the nearest doctor was miles away and refused to come for any money. So with the simple medical knowledge they possessed the parents did what they could and prayed almost unceasingly beside the cot and the crisis passed, and when he was slightly stronger they decided to risk carrying the baby to the doctor; and we have an account of that poignant journey written at the time by the mother. It is written for children, but it gives a clear description of the land in which they lived.

"*A Visit to the Doctor.* 'He is very pale, the little English baby,' thought coal-black Dinah, as she watched him carried past the door of her hut in his father's arms. The baby nodded gravely to black Dinah, and then watched the tiny white kids which were playing at her feet. It was dawn and the pasture of flowers lay drenched in deep dew, while the spiders' webs glistened like silver sheets. Baby was now just strong enough to be carried very gently the fifteen kilometers to the nearest doctor. The baby lived in a remote valley in the mountains, where the roads were sandy tracks or winding paths, with an occasional farm or hut made of mud and sticks.

"Baby never remembered having left the valley before; it was a great adventure and his big grey eyes looked out wonderingly from under the long, dark eyelashes, as he leaned over his father's shoulder. He felt no fear, for was he not in the strongest, tenderest arms in the world, and was not his mother just beside him on horseback? But there were a great many things to see, and he had no intention of sleeping.

"He watched the sunlight creeping down the mountain sides, chasing away the shadows, as it came steadily on, till all the world seemed bathed in the glorious flood of light. Daddy and he began to feel very hot, even under shady hats and a sunshade. The baby lived in Brazil and was not used to going out in the sun. Swarms of butterflies came out and danced and flitted about the flowers. Across the valley a soft brown oven bird was calling to his mate and a praying mantis beetle stood erect on a low rock as if to give thanks for the beauty of the dawn.

"Presently the little town came into sight, far below them, with the river foaming over the boulders in a mass of little cascades. An old wrinkled colored woman was washing clothes in the river and she called out as they passed, 'What a good husband,' and mother smiled and called back 'Yes, the best in the world.' And so after four hours they reached the doctor's house.

"Baby sat on the white table and played with the compass and watch his father gave him, while the strange man pulled him about and put queer things to his back and chest and throat and ears. And after it was all over he offered a wee thin hand to the doctor as if in acknowledgment of his attentions. Before he left, a very old Brazilian woman offered to heat his milk and took him and Mummy into her bedroom and showed them her saints and her pictures. She loved San Sebastian best. 'He is my Jesus,' she explained. She and Mummy had a long talk while baby lay and rested on her bed, and old Candida was very pleased to have a New Testament, of which she had heard, but which she'd never seen.

"When they set out for home, everything had changed. The air had that strange stillness only felt in the late afternoon. Children and babies, tired out with play, leaned against the walls of the huts. A very fat one of two, clad only in a rosary, lolled in a tiny chair with the air of a duchess.

"They went as fast as they could, for darkness would overtake them suddenly. Gradually the sky lit up with rosy clouds which changed to pale pinks and soon the short twilight was over. They had to go more slowly, but baby lay content, his eyes wide open, staring up at the first stars and watching the occasional flashes of lightning which lit up the path for an instant and showed the pale green leaves of the banana palms and the scarlet orange orchids that grew on the trees. Once it lit up a rough wooden cross, one of many in that district, put up to mark the spot where some traveler had died, sometimes by accident, sometimes by violence. On they went, the air now alive with night sounds, crossing streams, sliding down steep rocks, until at last they reached the home valley. The moon was up now, and they could see the leper's hut and the little shop; and then baby, sure of his bearings, slept soundly and did not stir when he was carried up the outside staircase to the little home under the roof and laid gently down in his cot."

So Farnham's life was spared, but he was still very weak, and a third child was expected in mid-April. Even their optimistic father realized that conditions were not suitable for delicate or new-born babies; and, besides, his first five years of service were up, and towards the end of February they said Goodbye to the sorrowing, loving group of Christians and set off to the coast, where they embarked for England. But they had left it rather late, and the storms were terrible. The new baby was very nearly born prematurely in the Bay of Biscay; but Ella survived and reached St. Leonards, where suitable arrangements could be made in plenty of time for the birth, which was expected in two weeks' time.

But she reckoned without her husband. Spring was in the air, and he was exuberant at being safe home in England with his family. They acquired a large, top-heavy pram for the two older children and went out for a family walk. He was not used to prams, for the roads round Carangola had been unsuitable for such vehicles, and at the top of a small slope he lost control. The pram careered to the bottom with Harold clinging on behind, but he could not stop it capsizing and pitching his babies out by the side of the road. They were quickly rescued, shaken but unhurt, but the shock had been too much for the mother at the top of the hill. She went straight back to the house and somewhat to her kind landlady's astonishment, Patricia Mary arrived a few hours later.

The family had six happy months in England together, and then Harold returned alone, leaving them in the home that Ella's mother had prepared for them. He missed them sorely, and his letters were full of his babies. He wrote on arriving back at the Bible School, "Just back from a walk to the dear old house. It made me feel very lumpy; I got right down under the house and imagined wee Puck in there playing. As I passed Leando's, he called me in to see his baby, eight months, very, very ill, and since then B. and I have been off and on just fighting for its life. I was looking at the skinny grey scrap yesterday and thinking of Tit (the third child) as I always see her, fat and bulging in woolly trousers, holding on to the cot rail, laughing all over her face, and quite indifferent to her Daddy's going away—a very picture of a baby."

"At last the mail. It gives me palpitation of the heart to see your fist. How darling of Farnham to take my photo to bed. I can just see the lamb in his dear nighty and his exquisite brown eyes."

"I am sending Pakita a birthday letter written on her fourth birthday. She's our special first, dearest baby.

"You are wonderfully near always, and I often look up and sort of expect you to come in with the babies. Tell me lots about them. They strike the native fancy hugely; everybody loves the photos, especially of Baby, so pert and fat and abundant-looking. Kiss each tiny scrap of the back of its neck. Isn't it awful I don't see Tit at this stage? I feel so pleased about her tooth. She's a prize baby."

"I delight in every detail. You make me see the nursery and each baby clearly, one by one. It's half the battle to see them in your writing. Wouldn't it be beautiful to give Puck to Zenana work, and perhaps the old gentleman to Africa?"

The "old gentleman" reached Africa, and Puck, as Principal of the British Lebanese Mission Training College for Girls Beirut, has helped to open the door of many an eastern home to the light of Christianity and education. But the seeds of missionary work were planted many years before by the lonely father in the Brazilian forests, and the mother who, inspired by a talk on the last chapter of Leviticus, on "Things devoted to the Lord," stood up at a Japan Evangelistic Band meeting when those who wanted to make an act of complete dedication were asked to rise. She very simply offered her three eldest (for the two youngest were not yet born) for the foreign field if God should so lead them. And the offering was accepted, for that was the attitude of those parents from beginning to end: their children were gifts to be brought up for God's service and to be given back to God as completely and unreservedly as possible. That, to them, was the underlying practical meaning of Psalm 84:3: "The altar is the only safe resting place for the heart's dearest affections; only completely yielded are they completely safe."

And while no children could have felt more loved and cared for, they knew instinctively that they were not the centre of the home, nor the first in their father's affections; and in this knowledge there was a kind of peace. To know oneself the centre and end of one's parents' existence may carry a certain responsibility too heavy and clinging for a dutiful child to bear. They knew without ever being told that the claims of God and His work would always be put first and there were certain limits of conduct beyond which they might never outwardly trespass, certain times and certain claims on attention on which they must never presume. It may sound a strain but it was not so; it was an atmosphere difficult to describe, but he unconsciously described it himself when speaking imaginatively in later years of the sojourn of the Ark in the house of Obed-edom.

"Now it is a very serious thing to bring the Ark of the Covenant into the center. A man was smitten to death and the Ark was swept aside into the house of an Edomite, and it stayed there for three months, and you can imagine the woman's fears—the mother with about seven or eight children—for there was that terrible blood-stained box, and the man who touched it fell dead, and here she is shut up in her cottage with her children and she says, 'How can I ever prevent their touching the Ark?' But as usually happens, all her fears turn out to be mistakes, and the blessing descended on that house so everyone was talking about it. There is a place where Christ is absolutely central, and such a change has come over those Edomite children; they are so easy to manage, and the house runs as if on oiled wheels. What has happened? Christ has got His place."

No one could say that the children were always easy to manage, but their father never realized it. He left the heavier side of their upbringing and all their serious training to their mother, never doubting for an instant that she was far more competent than himself in such matters. He was home seldom enough to see them through rose colored spectacles, and during his short visits the usual rules and regulations went west. They were riotous occasions of merriment—of being thrown out of bed in the morning, or listening to nonsense stories with a Biblical twinge on the Malvern Common. "There was once a striped tiger named Hezekiah, who ate fifty-seven bananas for breakfast every day, and he had a wife called Keren-Happuch."

There were games of bears under the nursery table, charades, camp fires, picnics, midnight feasts and long, long tramps fifteen or sixteen miles over the hills or to Upton on Severn. Yet this abandonment caused none of the usual disillusionment or unruliness that so often follows treats and irregularities; for he obviously considered them good children and, as children and many others will, they temporarily became what he thought them to be. Besides, he was so infectiously happy that no one wanted to spoil it by being naughty. Without a word on the subject he would leave them with the abiding impression that goodness was desirable, reasonable and utterly joyful, the only real fun in the world.

His influence over his children must have been largely unconscious, for he very seldom actually taught them anything at that age. Although he could speak delightfully to Sunday Schools on occasions, he did not consider himself gifted with children, and he left all the simplification of spiritual matters to his wife, of whose patient, thorough Bible teaching much could be written. She could come down to the level of the smallest, but he would retain his own level, only sometimes opening a door and allowing a little child to catch a glimpse of mystical glory far beyond it, and yet the more beautiful for being only vaguely understood, as when he lifted a seven-year-old daughter on to his knee and almost shyly, in a voice that sometimes trembled with emotion, read aloud all nineteen verses of Mrs. Cousin's hymn based on Samuel Rutherford's last sayings, "The sands of time are sinking, the dawn of heaven breaks."

And the result? The child was thrilled and transfixed. There was the feeling that Daddy had trusted her to share something that mattered to him, and there was a whole new world of bright imagery to explore and revel in, and eventually, after many years, to understand. In a surprisingly short time she had learned all nineteen verses off by heart, and the old Scottish divine might have smiled had he watched the brown little tomboy in the red bathing dress climbing a perilously steep waterfall in a stream bed and murmuring to herself:

> *Deep waters cross my pathway,*
> *The hedge of thorns was sharp;*
> *Now all these lie behind me.*
> *Oh, for the well-tuned harp.*

And in this combination of the mother's simple, straightforward teaching and the sense of the father's mysticism that was beyond them, there was a strength and a safeguard against the modern tendency, resulting perhaps from oversimplification of divine truth, to consider religion the property of the flannelgraph and the Primary Sunday School, and to abandon it at adolescence. To Mr. St. John's children, the knowledge of God was essentially an adult destination, beautiful as a golden sunset, where Father had arrived, and to which they might attain if diligent in the means of grace and lines of conduct which Mother had stayed behind to map out for them.

And it was necessary that someone should have stayed behind with them, especially at the Lord's Table, when Sunday by Sunday the five were led in, wriggling uncomfortably in the unaccustomed stiffness of Sunday clothes, all sharply on the look-out for anything that might prove even the least bit amusing, in order to beguile the rather warm, wearisome hour and a half ahead. It was necessary that someone should quell the ripples of delight that ran through the ranks when a cat strayed up the aisle and the old brother with the shaking hand endeavoured to catch it, or to check the silent mass hysteria that ensued when "the cock began to crow" was rendered as "the crow began to cock." Someone had to be on the spot to enquire why five-year-old Oliver was shaking with ill-concealed giggles over a reading in Colossians, and receive the whispered reply, "I never knew there was a book in the Bible called Goloshes!"—but that someone could never have been their father. He was completely oblivious of them—far, far ahead, seeing the realities hidden from them. They wriggled and yawned and diverted themselves with the last chapters of Job, which treated of the homely subject of birds' eggs, or acquainted themselves with Daniel's beasts or the less suitable stories in Judges, and they were often bored. But none of them looking at that rapt, shining, lifted face, or listening to that voice that trembled with adoring love, could maintain for a moment that the Breaking of Bread was really boring, and it left them with a feeling of mingled sadness and expectation: sadness because they were small and wicked and earthly and incorrigibly merry, and so could see nothing; expectation because they might some day grow up and understand and see what Daddy saw, and then, perhaps, that morning gathering would become the most wonderful place in the world—the very gate of heaven. And perhaps it was because of this that so much of their play centered round the story of King Arthur's Knights and the Holy Grail, and the character that one invariably impersonated in her lonely rambles and walks was that of Sir Galahad. What the Holy Grail was none of them knew; but one must be very pure in heart, like Daddy, to see it.

Yet though in their early childhood he very seldom consciously taught them anything, he had rigid principles as to the standards that he set, and the example he showed, and to this he often referred in his preaching. He condensed much of the spirit of those early years into part of a talk he once gave on the Songs of Degrees—"'Blessed is every-one that feareth the Lord; that walketh in His ways. For thou shalt eat the labour of thine hands: happy shalt thou be, and it shall be well with thee. Thy wife shall be as a fruitful vine by the sides of thine house: thy children like olive plants round about thy table.'

"How is a man to have all this stock of children and happy family life? In verse 3 you have the two parts as comparisons. The children are said to be like olive plants—they grow on the side of the hill, often out-side the house. But the wife is like a fruitful vine inside the house, for in the east the houses have courtyards and in the courtyards they train their vines. If they trained them outside everyone would steal them and the owners would get nothing, so they are in the innermost parts of the house. The Psalmist is old-fashioned to think that a woman's best place, if she can succeed in keeping it, is inside the house; very old-fashioned, but this Psalm was written a long time ago, and here's an exquisite picture of a Hebrew home in olden days.

"We are all sowers and builders for God, and the point of Psalm 128 is that we are essentially home-builders. This little group of Psalms deals with the simplest, most pedestrian things. You read of a man's daily work, of his life at home; and what does this business of home-building mean? The very least it means is that what we call religious life always moves in three circles—first the individual, private life with God; then the ecclesiastical, organized, Christian life, and behind the church and the heart there's always the Christian home. Nothing needs to be more safeguarded or attended to than the homes; for fathers and mothers are the responsible watchmen on the walls of the home. A mother came to me in America and said, 'Mr. St. John, I wish you'd speak to my children; my family's a shipwreck. My girl of twenty-one is trying to get her first divorce. My two boys are going to the devil as quickly as they can.' I said, 'Stop a moment and tell me, what was your home like?' She said, 'My husband and I have never been particularly religious people, but we've always been quite respectable.' I said, 'You were like the people round you twenty years ago, and you are surprised to find that your children are like the young people round them.' She said, 'My husband and I went to church one Sunday a month, but we went pleasuring the other three.' I said, 'I'll speak to your sons with pleasure, but I cannot do so with the slightest confidence. The Lord put you as the guardian of that home, and you were responsible to Him to bring up your children for God. They have seen that you don't really care for God at all. Are you surprised that your sons and daughters are exactly like you, merely with the slight outward change that people go further in this day than they did when you were young?'

"Take the Lord's Day, for instance. How many of the Lord's Sabbaths are described in the Gospels? You will find no less than nine. And how did He spend those days? He went about lifting the burdens from people's shoulders—it might be a case of dropsy, paralysis, curvature of the spine, the right hand withered. Wherever the Lord went He was always doing good. Was He at religious services all day? Not at all. In Mark 2 He went a nice country walk, not only for His own pleasure; He was helping His disciples, and as they walked they enjoyed heavenly things. I delight to read an account of one of the Lord's Sabbaths. It's a sheer delight to see Him in the morning in the Synagogue, in the afternoon in the house of a sick woman, in the evening sitting in the doorway and the people bringing their sick to Him, and if there's any spare time, a walk in the cornfields.

"In Luke 4 I read that Jesus, as His custom was, went into the synagogue on the Sabbath day; so don't let us think that an attendance at the Lord's Supper or at the various services, and our encouraging our children to follow in the road that we have walked in, are little things. For we have been given those dear homes that we cherish, where we have to set before our children examples, and as John Bunyan said, 'I was very careful to give my children no occasion, lest they should not be willing to go on a pilgrimage.'"

Not an easy thing to say, with a lynx-eyed son or daughter probably sitting in the audience weighing up every word; but in the matter of practising what he preached, he passed the test every time. In some ways he must have seemed a peculiarly indulgent parent, for he seldom corrected, although it must be added he knew that the mother did. With that sanity that so characterized him, he recognized himself as a man of God set apart, and of such, certain standards are required. He recognized us as ordinary, healthy children and of such certain other standards are required, and he never confused the species. Provided we were not malicious, he did not quell us when we mercilessly mimicked our elders and betters (and one or two of us were truly gifted in that direction), but *he* never spoke one discourteous or disrespectful word about anybody. We were left, within reason, to settle our disputes in our own rough and tumble way, but right up to the end we never heard a sharp, impatient, unloving word between himself and my mother. He encouraged us to enjoy ourselves and loved to give us treats; but we knew that he denied himself and kept under his body; and this positive, radiant holiness that went on its own way, seldom criticizing or scolding, was extraordinarily constructive and controlling. In that clear light the contrasts showed up too sharply. Small and sorry, we would sidle up to him, only to discover, as often as not, that our delinquencies had not been noticed at all. While we scrapped and scuffled, father had been thinking about the minor prophets!

CHAPTER 8

Father to the Multitude

WHAT do you know, my brethren, about caring for the young men? And you, my elder sister, what do you know about caring for your younger sisters in Christ? Have you made it your heart's business? I personally account it as one of my life's richest treasures that many young men, in many lands, are constantly writing to me about their souls' difficulties. I say God have mercy on the elder brother to whom his younger brethren do not come with their problems, their difficulties and their perplexities. And if you have spiritual travail for the souls of those who are young around you, you will find that they will flock up to you in the most amazing manner.

"What are those failings of which Paul and Christ spoke? Just this. For the sake of those who come behind, it is our business so to order ourselves that the young people who are always watching us with the most astonishingly keen eyes should never see in us anything that is un-Christlike or unlovely: that our words should be so weighed as though they were gold or silver, that we should keep clear of loose, thoughtless talking, that we should never allow a criticism of another Christian to pass our lips, lest our young people despise us.

"So let the Lord give us grace to have hearts for the young, and help us to walk before them in stainless, straight pathways, that as they watch us they may put their feet in the marks we have made in the sands of time. Many of us may have very little of life left to spend in His service. We are holding the vessels of the sanctuary, and the time will come when we must turn round and put them in the hands of younger men and women. Are we going to see to it that the hands into which we put them have been strengthened by the counsel we gave and words we spoke and even more than this, by the manner of men that we were?

"During the migration season on cloudy nights, many birds strike William Penn's statue in Philadelphia and fall dead on the ground. The keeper declares it is usually the young birds that fly too low that perish. Parents, pastors, teachers, teach your young to fly high! By example and by precept teach them to scale the heights, to breathe the rarefied air of God's atmosphere, for their soul's well-being."

(Extracts from Mr. St. John's sermons.)

As has been pointed out, Mr. St. John's influence on his small children was largely unconscious. He took little active part in their teaching and education, although much in their entertainment. But he prayed and planned for them, and he waited patiently for time and their mother to mould them, for he knew that one day his turn would come.

So while their mother mourned the passing of the years and the tumbling babies who seemed to turn into tough little boys and girls overnight, he exulted in each stage of their growth and bent his scholarly mind to each new achievement. He delighted in the exceedingly amateur family orchestra, and would become absorbed in a game of chess with a very small son. He would give the same concentrated consideration to the misspelled literary efforts of a little daughter as he would to his Greek commentary; in fact, he was the only person to whom she was not ashamed to show them.

"Don't you think daughters are lovely?" he once remarked, apropos of nothing at all; "so safe and satisfying."

So they grew and he watched and waited, never trying to force upon them the spiritual riches he had stored up for them until they were ready; and as there were no prodigies among them, they were well into their teens before they began to recognize the quality of his ministry or the peculiar sweetness of the Lord's Supper when he was present. But during their teenage years he baptized all five of them in the Gospel Hall at Cowley Road, Malvern, and began to introduce them to his own methods of Bible Study; and each one could testify that he opened up the Book to them as no one else had ever done, giving them hours of individual attention and teaching. Round about school-leaving age, the older children wanted to share these riches

HAROLD ST. JOHN with his grandson Paul,
taken in Tangier, 1952

with their friends, and for some years in the Easter Holidays we had what we called "The Applegarth Conference." To this lively group of young people he and the mother gave of their very best. Morning and evening sessions were given over to solid study and discussion, and the afternoon to wonderful picnics, rambles and high teas organized by the mother, who took the whole crowd of hungry, noisy creatures straight to her heart. They discussed their problems with Mr. St. John with unusual freedom because he was never shocked or surprised, and his humor, sympathy, sanity and broad understanding must have led many a rebellious, puzzled young Christian into right decisions and paths of peace. If they became particularly dogmatic and self-opinionated, he would preface his reply with such deliberate words as "My precious, noodle-pated, mug-faced, ranting idiot."

What was it that made his personality, counsel and teaching so intensely attractive to the young? Whether at home, or at the larger conferences, he was frequently the centre of a group of eager young men and women, or engaged in private session while one or another would lay bare his soul and talk unreservedly of his secret temptations. It may have been the absoluteness of his standards, or the superhuman demands he made on them; it may have been the tender humour and understanding with which he mingled these demands; it may have been his own humility. At all events, many hundreds of people wrote after his death from all parts of the world and from all spheres of life, to pay tribute to the profound influence he had had on them in their early years, and some of these are men and women who have become mighty leaders for God. "He did more to make Christ real to me than anyone else," wrote a missionary's wife in Rhodesia. "It is just wonderful to think that his joy, which is the biggest thing I remember about him, is absolutely free and perfect now."

"His influence over thousands is abiding today," wrote the Editor of *The Witness* who was one of Mr. St. John's dearest friends. "I owe an incalculable debt to him, and the increasingly close intimacy enjoyed during the last years has been one of the finest experiences of life. Everywhere I traveled, in North America and in the Antipodes, his name abides in fragrance, but in no heart will the memory be more revered than in my own."

"As far as we are concerned, our spiritual lives have largely been moulded over the years by his ministry," wrote another active servant of God.

"Your lectures have so colored my mind that you always seem with me interpreting when I read the Bible," wrote one of his own children in his twenties. "If you died, you'd never seem far away; I only have to go to the Bible to find you again."

Mr. Ransome Cooper wrote of him, "Mr. St. John's ministry has had a definitely formative effect on my character. He visited Liverpool when I was there and spoke on the wild ass that roamed where it would, untamed, with no bridle to its lusts. In well chosen words he applied the Scripture to several hundred young men crowded into the YMCA Hall for their Saturday evening rally. As he spoke of the need for a curb on our evil natures that longed to over ride our new redeemed natures and to lead us into sin, we had a glimpse of a wrecked Christian life unless we were kept by the power of God. I for one was deeply affected. Some of that holy awe at the thought of God's utter purity and the depravity of my own evil nature has remained with me."

"I was with him as a young man in the Bank," wrote another, "and his memory is fragrant. Unbelievers as well as believers spoke of him almost with reverence, because of his radiant happiness and readiness to help all and sundry. I can truly say he has had more influence on my life than any man I have ever met."

"I owe you something I can never repay—the means of my conversion," wrote one who knew him well in her girlhood. "With all my heart I thank God on every remembrance of you. Many a time I have weighed an action, or word, and thought, 'Well, I can't see Mr. Harry doing that.' I know the Lord is our pattern, but to see someone consistent is a check."

"It was always a great grief to us that he was unable to visit us again at our Conference Centre, as he was so effective with young people," wrote Mr. Tom Rees of Hildenborough Hall. "He had such rare understanding and specialized knowledge of so much in the academic field. He appealed to the simplest person, and yet the student who had intellectual difficulties found in Mr. St. John an expert who could answer his problems on his own intellectual level. He was also so down to earth on the practical problems of Christian behavior. There was nothing extreme or fanatical about his ideas. They were uncompromisingly spiritual, and yet never against common sense."

"I personally owe more to Mr. St. John's advice and sympathy than I can ever express," wrote a missionary in Spain. "To me he was a real spiritual father. I never met or knew of a more Christlike man, and how many thousands of believers and others feel the same."

In later years he never forgot the moods or restlessness of his own youth, and far from despising them, he saw in them a certain inevitable glory without which the world would be the poorer. Tenderly he dwelt on the meaning of the word "Youth" in an address given on Psalm 119 verse 9, in Wellington, New Zealand.

"I am going to run the risk of gravely offending my younger friends when I tell you what the word 'youth' means. First it means to shake up and down, then to rise up and down like a lion's mane. Jeremiah translates it 'to yell,' and the last interpretation means to throw yourself about on the floor. You young ladies will say, 'That does not describe me, I never throw myself up and down on the floor.' You are doing it all the time—I know what I'm saying for I'm not speaking to babies or little children, but to the class of people addressed in this verse, those who are passing from childhood to maturity. While you disdain physically to do the things that I have said, your whole life is one great interrogation point. You are as restless as youth always will be, challenging every thing you hear, and that is the quality and the province, and that is the essential glory of youth. It falls into despair, flings itself up and down, marches ahead in protest against unrighteousness and injustice. It has well been described as being a volcanic age, and what is a volcano but the protest of the inner forces of the earth against the crust that binds them? And when it ripples over the external crust of the earth you know it is only an internal protest coming to the surface. That is the supreme glory of youth—to protest against things, and the day may come when you will become cynical and too lazy to protest against anything. Keep your youth intact and the days of your youth virgin; all these glorious days when you don't know very much but think you know everything. The days when you have no colors in your painter's palette, and no hues on your canvas, saving the blue of the sky, and life is very, very good. So wherewithal shall youth find something that shall fall across the path of life and make it translucent?"

The skilful guide first lifts the eyes of his followers to some shining summit, and having thus gained their full inspired allegiance he then trains them in the practical humdrum technique of climbing. So Mr. St. John in the most solemnly worded appeals could move the hearts of his young hearers to a desire for a complete, high consecration, but he never left them with a sense of hopelessness or defeated impotence. Swiftly or in great detail, as time allowed, he would mark out the daily, practical habits by which their vow could be maintained: the right value of time, the use of recreation, regular church life, systematic giving, careful speech, self-discipline, reverence for the advice of older people, and, supremely, habits of prayer and methods of studying their Bibles; but of this last his teaching was so exhaustive that it requires a chapter to itself.

In how many hundreds of places the appeal to complete dedication rang out and found an answer in the hearts of young listeners whose attention had often first been gained by an anecdote! The following example is typical, too, of the way he often ended an address.

"I remember years ago in England I was staying near a large house in which the young heir, whose name was Arthur Scott, was celebrating his majority. His father gave a great party for his son's coming of age. Among his relatives was an old uncle, and the young man counted definitely on some handsome gift from him. Well, his uncle drove up to the house and said he would not stop to the ball but he would like to leave two envelopes for his nephew. 'One,' he said, 'you may open now; the other you must open alone, when you go to bed tonight.' The young man opened the first envelope and was very gratified to find a handsome check, and his fingers tingled to open the second, but he was sufficiently honourable to leave it as instructed. So he put it in his pocket and late that night in the silence of his bedroom he broke the seal, and to his surprise there was nothing in it but a little slip of paper with the words, 'To me to live is' and then a line. Young Arthur, whom I came to know very well later on, stood there looking at this piece of paper. He knew little of Scripture, but I have no doubt that the Spirit of God brought to his remembrance that there is one place in Scripture where it says, 'To me to live is Christ.' 'Now,' he said, 'I wonder why my uncle did not finish the verse. And in a flash he saw that it was a challenge, that every man can take five-sixths of the verse, but to only a few is the whole text available. 'To me to live,' you say, sitting here to-night 'is—what?—is to get on in business.' 'To me to live,' says a young man, 'is to get Mary Jane to be my wife.' 'To me to live is to be chosen in a certain football match with my picture in the papers.' It's going on all round us. To me to live is? Very well, are these the only answers you can give? Is there nothing better?

"Yes, there is that little Jew, sitting in prison, in bodily presence weak, in speech contemptible; scarred and maimed, having gone through thirty years of suffering for his Saviour. And there with the weight of the iron on his wrist, he writes the words painfully and slowly, 'To me to live is Christ.'"

"Shall it be so? Remember, here is no great gulf between the saved and unsaved. It's for every man to settle that question first—is it to be heaven or hell?—but when you've settled that question, the second one steps on the threshold and you cannot push it away. Not 'Is it heaven or hell?' any longer; is it heaven or earth? Are you going to live for time, and give your poverty to Jesus at the end, or will you say with simplicity and trust, 'Lord Jesus, I died with Thee, and I seek the things that are above; I set my heart on these things'? And if you do, you will find that all your life will be nourished by heavenly springs; Christ, your life, will be closer to you than breathing, nearer than hands or feet."

But having made these appeals, he would make it clear by precept and by example that such an act of dedication must color and affect every subsequent waking hour of a man's life. And how earnestly he entreated his young people to guard and discipline the use of their time. "We make that absurd excuse that we have no time to read our Bibles or to pray," he once cried, with that characteristic thump of his fist. "My dear young friend, you've got all the time there is. The Saviour once said there were twelve hours in the day; you tell me you have no time to read or pray. Remember this, twelve hours is a long time, and you can pack into twelve hours all that God meant you to do. And if He means you to pray there is plenty of time for it. Twelve hours a day, you say; from another angle that is extraordinarily few; often so few, I have no time to do anything much. Twelve hours!—plenty of time to do all God wants you to do. Twelve hours!—no time to do anything at all but what the Lord wants you to do. I am not greatly concerned if you do not have time to have your breakfast. I shall not be terribly upset if you cannot have your lunch, but I shall be broken-hearted if I think that you have no time to read your Bible and think of eternal things and serve the Lord."

This strong sense of the stewardship of time deeply affected his ideas on young people's recreation, and they flocked to him to hear his views on the subject of so-called "worldliness." "What harm is there?" they would ask, and that was a question he would never answer, for he could never bring himself to deal much with negatives. Everything in him was positive, and he would parry with the energetic counter-question, "What good is there?" "Young men," he would say, "often consult me as to the desirability of a certain habit; young women occasionally write to me concerning some modern custom about which they seem uncomfortable. 'Why do you do it?' I ask, and if the reply is 'Because I like it,' or 'Because other girls do it,' then I should enquire whether 'I like' is ever laid down in Scripture as the guiding rule for believers. And again whether we want to flatter the world by paying it and its votaries the compliment of imitation. These matters are perfectly simple. If the Lord has laid them on your heart as something to be done to His praise, then set about them with energy and purpose of heart; if not, leave them severely alone until He awakens some exercise in that direction."

Yet it was a subject on which he seldom touched, and then never in detail unless asked. He would not lay down the law, but when challenged he would suggest questions, often in a half-humorous vein, to which each conscience must give its own answer before God. He told once of how he was crossing the campus of one of the American Bible Schools, when he noticed a group of about fifteen young people gathered under a tree arguing with great energy about some matter. "One of them, a fair fluffy little thing of about sixteen, caught sight of me and called me over to ponder a great problem, and she said, 'Now, Mr. St. John, do you think a young Christian should dance?' I replied, 'First of all, I'm glad you say a *young* Christian. An old Christian doesn't want to, his bones are too stiff. Now you've asked me a very great question and it's much too hard for me to answer! If you'd asked me something simple, like the meaning of Ezekiel's wheels, or the wings of the seraphim, I could have told you at once, but to a question as deep as that I must say, I cannot answer you!' And there were fifteen disappointed faces. 'But I'll tell you what I can do—I'll help you to answer your own question, each one for himself.' So getting a piece of paper I drew a line down the middle of the centre, and in the centre I put a cross; so there was the blank sheet of paper with the sign of the Cross in the centre. And I wrote on this side 'B.C.' and on the other 'A.D.' 'Now,' I said, 'on that sheet of paper everything on the left hand will be what is suitable to the days before you knew Christ, everything on the right hand suitable to the days after you knew Christ. Very well, I shall say a few things, and you will sign with your hand, left or right.' I began throwing out words very quickly—sport for exercise, prayer meetings, this and that; and about the twelfth thing I threw out was dancing, and like a flash they all signalled the left side. When the question was put suddenly, they knew, instinctively.

"And I make bold to say," went on Mr. St. John as he told of the incident, "that when you come to questionable things you can nearly always settle them by writing B.C. or A.D. Do they really suit Christ? Can He smile upon them? Can you seek His favor on them? If not, you dare not do them. And there are certain deep, stable instincts that God has put into our lives as Christians and it is well for us never to violate them. Our business is to walk in separation from this present world. Now I'm not going to give you any broad or narrow interpretations of that. You may enjoy beautiful things and the Lord Jesus never took from anybody any single thing that was good. If you think that becoming a Christian means you must give up good things, it's a lie. He never took a good thing from anybody. He took the corrupting things, the things that lessen, the things that are base and common, but He never took a thing that would honor or bless His Name."

Very narrow according to modern ideas, but it was the narrowness of the captured heart that had known the length and the breadth and the depth and height, and sought nothing outside or beyond. His standard was one of unreserved, single minded devotion to Christ in every detail of life. Simple, because it admitted of no exceptions and made no allowances, and hundreds of young people heard the call and flocked to the standard.

How then did he counsel the young men and the young women of his time to spend their leisure hours? He advised them to live normal, healthy lives, and to enjoy every activity where Christ might be included and to shun every activity where He would not be welcome. Social intercourse he considered was good and helpful, but he deplored the hours wasted among Christians in aimless small talk. "In your church life," he pleaded, "see that you cultivate spiritual not social relationships. For relationships that are merely social can be a curse to the church; spiritual ones are an unmixed glory and blessing. I mean this: when you young women visit each other, carry a Testament in your pocket, and when you've heard about Mrs. Jones's baby, or Miss Smith's affairs, draw out your Testament and say, 'Here's a precious word I've received from the Lord this morning,' and then you two young women can bow together in prayer, and as you go home down the street you will have left a benediction in your track. And you young men, when you come together in the evening, get together over the Scriptures. I well remember the days in my own home when servants of Christ came to visit us, and we loved to see them open the Scriptures and give us about ten minutes or so of well-chosen instruction when the meal was over. I remember in my youth how twenty or thirty of us would gather in some quiet village for a week of our summer holidays and from 9:00 to 12:00 each morning we would study the Scriptures, and in the evening we would go out and speak in the open air, giving our afternoons to proper exercise to keep our bodies fit vessels. Never will I forget the joy with which we explored those golden fields of Scripture."

"I well remember when I was first saved," he said on another occasion, "I went for a walking tour with a young man, older than myself, but what struck me about this young man was that, when we reached some out-of-the-way village, the first thing he did was to go and hunt up some of the Lord's people. I shall never forget the joy I had in the companionship of that young man whose first concern was to go and find the Lord's people."

To him a Christian was a Nazarite—set apart; an athlete, unencumbered; and just as he bade young disciples steer clear of all pastimes and recreations which they could not share with their Master, so he urged them to travel light and to beware of the distractions and entanglements of increasing worldly possessions. His was a lonely voice in this age of increasing comfort and materialism, but it was typical of the man that he would set off on a journey half round the world with no more than he could carry in his hand. Self-denial, contentment, and simplicity in the material realm were qualities that he considered essential in a man of God.

"Wesley went into business on £30 a year," he once said, "and he decided the Lord should have £2 and John Wesley should have £28. The next year his master said, 'John, you've been a good servant, I must double your salary.' Magnificent—here is £32 for the Lord. The next year, so says the diary, it's £120—wonderful, still £28 for John Wesley, £92 for the Lord. And that was the way John Wesley lived. Now, says Paul, I have a perfect right to do what I like with my money and my family; let no man tamper with my freedom, but the moment I have asserted it, I surrender it for Christ's sake."

And always as he looked out on a company of young men and women, the need of the mission field and the Lord's last command to evangelize the world rose before him. But he was never one to push candidates out lightly into the field, or to work on their emotions. "What is your attitude, in view of the Lord's return, to this most tremendous and important service?" he would ask. "You younger men and women, do give careful, extensive study to these problems, and understand the things that our missionaries fight against. Do you see to it that your prayer is consistent? If so, there will be a regular taking up of one of the various printed prayer lists, and you will give yourself in definite intercession. And then prayer and interest shall merge into a third thing—that is sacrificial giving, giving that costs and means self-denial: perhaps the wearing of a garment twice the ordinary time, the surrender of some of those things to which we are accustomed; but anything that is of a sweet savor of Christ must be that which has cost us something—the self-denial that strips itself of things to which it is entitled, in order that for Christ's dear sake we may be able to care for those representing Him and working for His sake in the service of the gospel. And if by His help we have learned to study and to pray and to give, it may be that He will put out His hand and select us as missionaries to go far afield. But remember, He's not very likely to select you unless every ounce of your love and devotion has been flung into His service."

"Has the young applicant supported the mission field with prayer and sacrificial giving? Has he studied the subject? Has he been a missionary in his own district?" And even when satisfied on this count, from his own experiences in many mission fields, he still feared for the consequences of immaturity.

> The priests cannot commence until they have attained thirty years of age, because they represent Christ in His highest offices for God and for men. (See in Numbers chapter 4 the phrase "From thirty years old and upwards" occurring seven times, and compare Luke 3:23, when the accepted Priest stands in Jordan, being about thirty years old.) The Church has often overlooked these distinctions and thus the cause of Christ has been gravely weakened by our self-will. "Not a novice" (Greek—a newly implanted soul) says the inspired Word. But still we persist in sending forth untried, untaught young men and women to man the mission field and to guide the destinies of infant churches. Is it any wonder that our progress is erratic and slow?
>
> In contrast, in Numbers 1:5-16, a five-fold description is given of those who are chosen for service, and each suggests a distinct qualification for church leadership:
>
> a) They stand with Moses as men unswayed by human influence, their eyes fixed on Christ the Mediator (v.5).
>
> b) They are renowned, literally "the summoned ones," called to lead in assembly matters because it is recognized that they are men of spiritual worth (v. 16).
>
> c) They are princes, from the verb "to exalt," and thus remote from the crowd of lesser men.
>
> d) As heads of thousands they are accustomed to command (v. 16).
>
> e) They are expressed by name (v. 17). This last phrase is literally "those whose names are pricked or pierced." In olden days parchment rolls were kept on which were written the names of citizens and land-owners. When sheriffs were to be selected, the king would look down the list, and with a bodkin he would pierce the parchment against the names of those who were counted fit to hold office.

Many a young man or woman consulted him and prayed with him, and some may have wavered at the absoluteness of his demands. Were they prepared to subordinate marriage, or to postpone it, if it should stand in the way of their call or impair their usefulness to the Lord's work? And if not, had they really received a call at all? "I have had a great deal to do in the last forty years with young missionaries," he said, toward the end of his life. "I am sure that the marriage question handled in the light of their own desires rather than in the light of the Lord's will has ruined, shortened and weakened the testimony of countless young missionaries. There is the feeling that it's very nice to have someone by your side to hold your hand when you're feeling depressed, and they often rush into marriage; and the next thing is, their efficiency is impaired and they cannot travel freely; they are bound and tied within certain very narrow limits. But if the Lord ever calls you to whole-time Christian service, settle it in your soul first of all whether the Lord's work would be best helped in this condition or in that one, and not what your desires are, or what seems best to the proposed partner of your life."

But, having assessed their zeal in the Lord's work, their maturity and their devotedness, he had statesmanlike theories on their designation.

Our Lord is an accurate architect. He is a far-sighted general. Are we all satisfied that our foreign legions and our home base are working together as He would wish? When the historian Gibbon offered his five reasons for the success of primitive Christianity, he cited the following features of the work:

The early believers were distinguished by
a) The simplicity and certainty of their belief in God and in miracles.
b) The austerity and purity of their morals.
c) Their unity and mutual affection.
d) Their fiery zeal for God and man.
e) Their statesmanship in planning new work.

Let us look at the earliest records available:

1) Christ loved the world and heard the sobbing of its millions, but He limited His services to one tiny Roman province, winning in all about 500 adherents.
2) The twelve apostles started from a center, and gradually widened out as assemblies grew in numbers.

3) Paul, the pioneer, flung forth his carefully drawn lines along the main Roman roads, planting churches as he went, planning constant visits to those among whom he had labored.

4) The Lord in His glorified ministry sent out letters to seven churches in Asia Minor, and we note that the cities named were the main posting stations on a circular Imperial highway.

Surely we may learn much from these facts, and in the little future which may be left to us, let us look ahead and build wisely, well, and truly.

Deeply concerned as to the quality of the young people sent out, urging them to count the cost to the uttermost, yet occasionally carried away by the vision, he would use all his eloquence to portray the need and to stir the hearts of his hearers to face the challenge. In an article in *The Bible Scholar* he closed with the following anecdote:

"Two scraps of Scripture set side by side may serve to illumine what is in my mind.

"'The children of Israel sighed.'

"'And Moses kept the flock of his father-in-law.'

"We are surrounded by a sighing world and millions are calling to us for the light. It's true that some must tend the flocks at home. Keeping sheep is excellent work, but not for a man like Moses. To succeed in business, to excel in a profession is pleasant, but is that the will of Christ for you?

"I remember hearing a nurse from Japan telling of an experience in a children's ward in her hospital. Like most missionary institutions it was disgracefully under staffed, and she was wrestling with the work of four nurses. Passing down the ward she heard a little yellow-skinned boy of about eight moaning in fear and crying, 'Nurse, it's very dark, very dark.' Her impulse was to leave all and sit with him during the few hours that remained to him of life, but that was impossible. She could only turn aside for a moment, whisper a few words about the Good Shepherd, and hasten to other sufferers. You see, the little Japanese boy sighed, while some Christian nurse kept the flock at home.

"An hour later she passed the bed again and heard the low, terror-stricken cry, 'Nurse, it's very dark, very dark.' Still just one word of comfort, and then fresh calls. You see, the little Japanese boy cried, while some Christian nurse kept the flock at home.

"The third time she crossed over to the cot and as the child slipped away into eternity he muttered, 'Dark, dark.' So the little Japanese boy died, and the Christian nurse kept the flock at home.

"Are you that nurse?"

And to many dark, lonely places of the earth, his letters followed these young missionaries and cheered them. Completely devoid of banalities or small talk, he would pierce to the heart of the matter in weighed, pithy words, lifting it up to the light of God.

"God keep you," he wrote to a missionary working in an isolated, discouraging station, "and make you like Noah's ark, pitched without and within, invulnerable to dampened spirits or to the blistering weariness of the way; and like the golden ark with the wings of God spread over you, with His law of love hidden in your heart."

And again, to one who he suspected was over-working and neglecting his spiritual life, "I notice the laws as to the priest's clothing in Ezekiel 42:13 and 14. They go dressed in fair white linen to share the most holy things, but they come out to meet men in common raiment. They scale heights with God and feel that to gain His presence is worth no little trouble. Again in chapter 44:17-19, in the inner court they allow no heat or haste, no sweat; they will not gird themselves with wool. (Deut. 22:11—no mingling of worldly comforts with the righteousness of saints.)

"There must always be the two courts in life, the outer where we deal with life's duties, the inner where we enjoy Psalm 27:4."

To one who was grieving because her activities had been checked by Government regulations: "If we look at the Government action we may become bitter. If we only look at the movement of the hand of God our hearts become soft and tender, and we remember that, if an under-shepherd is transferred to another piece of work in the factory of the Father, the Chief Shepherd can well care for the little flock."

To one whose way was dark and uncertain: "What a rest it is to have certainties in an uncertain world. I KNOW—WE KNOW—YE KNOW (2 Tim. 1:12, Romans 8:22, 1 John 2:20-21), and because we know we can pray, 'Lord, lead me to the other side of darkness,' or, if we were up to it, 'into the thick darkness where God is' (Exodus 20:21). It is not a vacant or lonely darkness for He is there."

To one fearful on account of the political future: "If only people knew that God has set His Son in Zion, and that His prophetic timetable is fixed and will be carried out as punctually as a Bradshaw's Timetable! I like to think of Christ in a peasant's dress standing on the Mount of Olives and publishing his plans for the future of Europe, and knowing that though heaven and earth shall dissolve, His Word shall stand."

To one who had to make a decision: "I am heavily and happily burdened for you. The branching road of your immediate future stretches ahead of you and you will have to make a decision ere long. Till that hour comes keep an open mind hospitable to the truth as it comes to you, an open heart ready to entertain the demands of love and its rights, and an open hand prepared to give and serve."

To one of his daughters, abroad: "I have been feeling deeply the checks and disappointments of your service, the apparent triumphs of Satan. M's failure, R's sin, H's instability. All have burdened me deeply, but I try to set them in the light of Psalm 90, verse 4—our long millenniums of tears and patience and toil set in perfect proportion in a few hours; or think of Peter's addition—one of our short days lengthened out into long centuries of blessing or otherwise. Hagar enters the tent of Abraham, and today three hundred million Moslems stand in serried ranks of opposition to God's cause as the result of one man's momentary weakness. But thank God that's only half the truth. Jesus Christ has a few minutes with Saul of Tarsus, on the road to Damascus, and a broad new stream flows into the river of God and it still keeps its beauty of color, like the blue Rhone mingling with the muddy Arve. Work on, and keep your dear, fair head above the stream. You shall reap if you faint not."

To a son: "God keep you very strong, very firm, very close to your resting place. The Cross is the resting place for sin, the tomb for self, and the throne for our fears."

And occasionally there would be a few lines in a lighter vein, like the inscription stuck on the top of an oil stove for his daughter who was spending the winter up on the cold Moroccan mountains:

"She spreadeth out her hands to the poor; yea she reacheth out her hands to the needy. With her new stove she is not afraid of the snow" (Proverbs 31:20 and 21).

CHAPTER 9

The Traveler

WHEREVER God walks He always leaves a blessing. How many of us sometimes leave nothing. Some leave a curse or a blight, but every time—speaking with reverence—God goes out walking, He leaves a blessing." (Commentary on the verse "All thy paths drop fatness.")

As a traveling Bible teacher, Mr. St. John spent about forty years of his life mostly in travel, and his ministry extended to North and South America, the West Indies, Europe, North and South Africa, Palestine, Australia and New Zealand, and wherever he went men and women and children bore witness that, like his Master, he too had left a blessing.

"His influence on people was very great indeed," wrote one who often ministered with him. "In my travels I have met many men who are now leaders among God's people, whose lives were touched by him at a crucial time. I have talked of him with such men as Walter Munro of New York and Don Parker of the same city, both spiritual leaders, and both of them affected by contact with him when he used to visit the USA regularly in the 1920's. I found H. C. Hewlett of Palmerston North, New Zealand, to be another whose life was touched and profoundly influenced by Mr. St. John when he first visited New Zealand in 1934 and again in 1937. He told me that such ministry had never been heard in New Zealand and people flocked from every side to hear him. Whenever he spoke, the building would be crowded to capacity, people traveling many miles to attend the meetings. What he did for the young men of those assemblies was to give them standards they had not known before, and which many of them sought to attain in their personal ministry."

"Wherever I have traveled, in England or USA," said another, "I have heard Mr. St. John's ministry spoken of with deep appreciation.

He was loved everywhere, not only for his teaching, but for the charm of his Christian character."

Yet at first sight there was nothing particularly striking or impressive about the traveler who set off across oceans and continents, carrying a small shabby bag in each hand, containing the minimum of clothing and the maximum of books, a Bible or commentary bulging from his pocket. He never could take his belongings very seriously, apart from books, and was frequently leaving them behind, until in desperation he gave up wearing a hat altogether. His wife would write many letters in her attempts to track his belongings and was usually successful. Her children remember her merriment when, hoping to retrieve an almost new pair of trousers, she received a letter from the States which started "Dear Bro., Pants to hand."

He would board the train at Malvern, with his hair on end after the hugs of five lamenting children, and would go off waving an umbrella which he invariably lost within the first few days of his journey. He seldom indicated the exact time he would arrive anywhere, for he could not bear anyone to take the trouble to meet him at the station; and although he tried to warn his family of the hour of his return, he occasionally raced his own letters. There is a memory of him walking up from the Malvern Station after nine months' absence and meeting his son, in a pram which looked vaguely familiar. He hovered doubtfully for a moment or two, and then addressed the girl in charge.

"Excuse me, but is this by any chance my baby?"

The girl, who was new and nervous, replied, "I'm sure I couldn't say, Sir."

Yet there were some who traveled with him who looked twice. It may have been the obvious happiness of the man, or the old-fashioned courtesy with which he would stand aside or leap to his feet to offer his seat to a lady. Whatever it was, those who took time to observe him were strangely drawn to him, sometimes without knowing why.

"Who was your friend walking down the street with you?" asked a young doctor in Belfast of one of his medical colleagues. "He had the face of a saint."

"May I presume to speak to you without introduction, on the basis that we are both British people in a foreign country?" asked an English lady, staying in the same hotel in Rome.

"Certainly, Madam," he replied.

"I want to ask you a personal question," she said. "Will you please tell me the secret of your serenity? For two days I have been watching you and I can see that you live in a different world from mine." This led to a conversation that ended in the lady accepting his Lord as hers.

And to those who loved the Lord he was easily recognizable as a fellow-lover. He often told how he was traveling in the Underground when Mr. Hubert Verner of the Japan Evangelistic Band, a man with that same luminous quality of radiance, boarded the carriage a little further down the train. The men had never met, but they noticed each other instantly and finally managed to get close to each other, drawn by some mysterious bond of common love.

"I believe you know a Friend of mine," said Mr. St. John simply, and in a moment they were rejoicing more than ever when they disclosed their identities, and Mr. Verner drew a little notebook out of his pocket and showed the names of Mr. St. John's five children written inside.

"Your wife put me up when I was speaking at the Malvern Keswick Convention," he said. "I grew very fond of those five little children. I've prayed for them each by name every day since, and I have always longed to meet their father."

So the Underground roared on its way, but a corner of that noisy carriage was a second road to Emmaus, where the hearts of two of Christ's lovers burned within them, as He drew near and went with them. One cannot help wondering whether Mr. St. John, at least, remembered to alight at his destination.

To him no journey was merely a means of getting from one place to another but a fresh opportunity of speaking of Christ. Never indiscriminate or aggressive, he had a rare gift of getting into conversation with his fellow-travelers—on board ship often through a game of chess. And people would unburden themselves to this man who seemed so at leisure from himself and so sincere in his sympathy. He would listen quietly, waiting that touch of the Spirit on the conversation that showed that the moment was ripe to speak of spiritual things. Amused his hearers may sometimes have been, but never offended or put off; and many a soul found peace in a ship's saloon, in the railway carriage, or by the roadside. Any place to him was a sanctuary, and to a lady who once objected that if they knelt to pray in a hotel lounge people might come in, he replied that it did not matter, because as soon as anyone realized that they were praying, they would go away—which they certainly did!

His own accounts of some of these conversations are interesting.

"I was standing by the side of the road not long ago with two heavy bags. There were no buses and I was about a mile and a half from the Conference which I wished to attend, so I asked the Lord about the matter and told Him my position; and just as I was telling Him, a man drew up and said, 'Excuse me, can you tell me where such and such a place is?' I said, 'It is three miles up the road,' and he looked at me and said, 'Can I give you a lift?' 'Thank you,' I said, and after I'd been in the car a few minutes, I said, 'Do you know what I thought of as I got into this car? It's a word in the old Book that says, "Bear ye one another's burdens, and so fulfil the law of Christ." Do you know anything about that?' He stopped the car, swung round on me and said almost fiercely, 'Why do you say that word out of the Bible to me? The last time I was in church sixteen years ago the minister preached on that text, and I've never darkened the door of a church since.' 'Well,' I said, 'what was wrong with that Scripture?' 'Oh,' he said, 'he read the beginning of some chapter, "Bear ye one another's burdens," and then he read almost in the next verse, "Every man shall bear his own burden," and I asked the clergyman what he meant by those verses, and he said he didn't know.'

"'Very well,' I said, 'we will look it up for one moment. For there are two words for burdens. The first, in the verse "Bear ye one another's burdens," means a load under which a man is staggering. It is a simple exhortation to kindness, to do as Christ did. In the next verse the word "burden" is a nautical word, the word sailors use; it's used of the cargo of a ship. Now a ship's captain never wants anyone else to carry his cargo for he would lose all his profit. And that means that everyone must carry his own burden of responsibility.'

"'Is that really right?' he said.

"'Yes,' I answered, 'and doesn't that look as though the Book is not so stupid as you thought? Now you just drive up to that place where

I'm going and we'll sit down in a quiet corner and we'll go over those sixteen wasted years and I'll tell you what the Lord Jesus has done for me and what He can do for you.' So there we sat for nearly an hour in a side road, and I preached to him Jesus. And I gave you that illustration to show you that you meet the strangest, most out-of-the-way people, and thousands of them, literally thousands, are ready, if we will only preach to them of the wisdom of Christ. It is extraordinary to see how grateful people are that someone takes an interest in a stranger's soul. Let the redeemed of the Lord say so, for the sake of the people around who are dying without Christ. We know we're out of the desert, and they don't; we have the key to the dungeon, and they haven't; so for our own sakes, for their sakes, and for His sake, let us say so."

"It has been borne upon me," he said on another occasion, "in hundreds of recent contacts with men and women in this world, that there's a tremendous eager enquiry in the hearts of countless men and women. Behind barriers of reserve, sometimes behind barriers of blasphemy, there's a profound hunger for certainty in heavenly things. Some time ago in Gloucestershire, I met a woman wheeling a bicycle piled high with Sunday papers, and as she was at the bottom of the hill I offered to wheel it for her. She said, 'Thank you, I'm going downhill,' along a turning I hadn't noticed. I handed her a gospel booklet, and she lingered for a moment or two, looking steadily at me, and with a voice and manner quite different from what I expected, she said to me, 'I wonder if you could spare a corner in your prayers for a seller of Sunday newspapers?' I said, 'Of course I could, and I will, but tell me about yourself—why are you doing this?' She said, 'I suppose you're going to the little hall in the village to preach today.' 'Yes,' I said. 'Well,' she said, 'I used to go there and played the harmonium and was very happy; but I was poor, and someone told me there was a big profit to be made from Sunday newspapers, so I took on the work, and I've made a deal of money and never known a day of happiness since I started.' And as she mounted her bicycle she looked back and said, 'I wish you'd find a corner in your prayers for a seller of Sunday newspapers!'"

He could not bear any slight or carelessness in connection with the Name he loved. When he was traveling in a bus in Lanarkshire in Scotland a fellow passenger broke into blasphemous talk. Mr. St. John went up to him at once and with real sorrow, yet without anger, told him he had spoken evil of his best Friend. The man was completely broken down by this approach and made a sincere apology before leaving the bus.

On another occasion he was standing in the private chapel of Keble College, Oxford, lost in contemplation of Holman Hunt's masterpiece, "The Light of the World." A chattering party of tourists approached and the guide announced in a strident voice: "The original of this picture was sold for £5,000." Without a moment's hesitation, Mr. St. John stepped forward. "Ladies and gentleman," he said, "may I add that the true original of this picture was sold for thirty pieces of silver." A hush fell on the crowd, and they left the chapel in silence.

Another friend remembers him standing in a bus queue followed by a family. When the bus arrived there was room for everyone except the father. The conductor tried to prevent the man from boarding the bus, stating that standing was forbidden. The man maintained that his wife and children were aboard and therefore he would not dismount. The conductor called the driver and a heated argument ensued; both declared that the bus would not start until the man had alighted.

In the angry silence that followed Mr. St. John rose to his feet and addressed officials and passengers: "Ladies and gentlemen," he said in his inimitably courteous manner, "it looks as though we shall all be late home. The conductor's perfectly right, for he's supporting his own bye-laws; the passenger is also right for he's supporting an older law of humanity, which forbids separating a man from his family. I can see no way out except for me to give up my seat to the gentleman, and then alight and wait for the next bus, and then everyone will be satisfied and you will all get home. But before I get off, may I add one thing? This is exactly what my blessed Saviour, the Lord Jesus, has done for me. He has given me His place in light and salvation, and on the Cross He took my place as a sinner in death and darkness." As he swung off the bus Mr. St. John heard the conductor saying, "Ain't he a rum bloke?"

Perhaps another reason why he felt so at home with all ages and creeds and classes in so many parts of the world was his willingness to give and take, never despising anyone. "There were two men who taught me more of the things of God, as a young man, than any others," he once said. "One was a miner who probably earned a very low wage, and the other was a peer of the realm. I used to sit with each of these hour after hour." A friend recalls an incident when, during his travels, he visited a house where one of the kings of Europe was a guest, and Mr. St. John, completely at ease, led the conversation round to spiritual matters, and in the end the king accepted a Bible.

He could stand and teach a king; equally at his ease, he could sit in the dust and learn from a savage. He himself gave the following account of a meeting in the wilds of Somaliland.

"I was sitting once in Somaliland in a Post Office, and you must not imagine a magnificent building like that in Wellington. It was a small tin shack with a floor inches deep in dust, and a little wooden box with a lot of dusty letters in it. Well, I managed to get the use of one of these Post Offices for a Bible Reading, and we had seven or eight fine Somalis. I won't say anything about their clothing, but one man was wearing a leopard skin and he'd been named "2 1/2 pence." He didn't know what it meant, so it didn't matter; and during the meeting I looked across at him and said without a smile, 'Dear brother 2 1/2 pence, have you any thought as to why the Scripture tells us that the soldier plunged his lance into the Saviour's side and there came out blood and water?' And that untutored savage, who had only known his Saviour for a short time, and emerged from the most degraded heathendom, gave an answer that could never have been bettered by any theological college in the kingdom. He said, 'My white brother, I suppose it was that all the world might see that by the death of the Saviour a highway had been opened right up to the heart of God.'"

A real citizen of the world, he must have stayed in thousands of homes in different lands, and many can look back and thank God that ever he turned aside to sojourn with them. "He was a perfect gentleman in any situation," wrote one of his hosts. "I have lived with him in other people's houses and he was an example to all itinerant preachers of decorum, friendliness, helpfulness. It was nothing for him to go into the kitchen and wash up the dishes. I have been with him in the house of mourning, and his kindly sympathy and loving tact taught us who were younger how to act in such circumstances."

For one thing he was always anxious to meet the children, probably a rare taste in one who often had two or three heavy meetings a day, but nevertheless a key to a mother's heart. But perhaps for the sake of the five at home they drew him irresistibly, and he them.

"Where are the children?" he suddenly asked at the close of a meal in a home in Scotland. It was supposed they'd slipped away to do their homework, but it was snowing hard and Mr. St. John caught a glimpse of them through the window. He was out in a moment, in the thick of a snow fight. It was two girls and a boy against the preacher, but they were a match for each other both in strength and in glowing enjoyment.

They flocked to him wherever he went, and there is a memory of him at one of the last Grittleton Conferences, sitting with little Hilary Pope on his lap, imagining himself unobserved. What were they so absorbed in, the white-haired saint and the curly baby? An onlooker approached softly and heard the following, interrupted at the end of each line by peals of baby laughter:

> *Sing a song of. . . Threepence-halfpenny,*
> *A Pocket full of. . . oats,*
> *Four and twenty. . . robins,*
> *Baked in a. . . pudding.*

And on those little children in whose homes he visited he left an abiding impression. There is a precious letter to hand that tells of a little girl, Ethel Gray, who, over forty years ago, used to sit on the stairs with her sisters and wait for his coming. "Of course we were only children at the time, but how great can the influence of a good man be on the life of a little child. On thinking it over, while reminiscing on that great Christian gentleman, Mr. St. John, it came to me that I owed to him a great deal more than I realized. It was when I was about six that I remember him, and certain scenes form an integral part of my childhood background. We were living in Buenos Aires at the time and Mr. St. John visited us on Sunday—at least I think it was Sunday; any day of the week felt like Sunday when he was around, and his visits were prized by us children as though he was our special visitor. We called him 'our Mr. St. John.'

"We would gather, three of us, aged between four and seven, round the top of the iron staircase that led to our floor, and wait there for his footsteps. The first to hear it announced in ringing tones, 'Mr. St. John,' and then our hands would be clinging to his trousers, escorting him to the dining room. I remember him next at table; he was so quiet, so gracious, so courteous. My place was opposite his and I observed, as a child will, every movement. Unconsciously, his example became engraved on my mind, and it is in this that his influence has had the greatest power over me. He made us mind our manners, and I saw how he rose to open a door, to set a chair, how mother came first; I noticed that his voice never rose, his movements were gentle, he never contradicted; and a thousand more little things. Our love for him made him a person to live up to, and many a time in later years I've wondered to myself, reviewing my life, among the poorest communities, from where I got my concept of the English gentleman and Christian courtesy. And now I realize it was from Mr. St. John. He devoted a part of his visit exclusively to us, and taught us little choruses, and set us Scriptures to memorize. He always brought some little package to mother containing some dainties that made Sunday tea special. But there came a Sunday that was to be his last, and there was a little package for each of us. We glanced at mother and she nodded permission, and I recall that she looked very touched as we each unwrapped our own—a tiny china teaset, a little doll; even the baby had something.

"We never saw him again and we missed him terribly; his name was a household word and 'Mr. St. John says,' and 'Mr. St. John does' were constant references. Yet as the years went by and his memory became almost legendary, his physical presence faded but his example sank deeper and deeper into our consciousness so that habits of gentleness and courtesy and God-fearing obedience were formed and retained."

To him each little child was of infinite importance, and there is a story told of how he took the small girl of the house for a walk in a golden autumn forest in North America. Sitting on a fallen log he picked up an exquisitely tinted leaf, and with his arm round the child he traced the story of the leaf from Spring to Autumn, the drawing in of sunshine and rain, and the giving out of such beauty in its dying, and the child said, "I understand what you mean; when I'm little I must take in every good thing I can get, and when I'm old I shall give it all out again, in happiness and goodness."

"Dear Mr. St. John, he was all silver to me as a child—silver hair, silver voice; I can hear it now," wrote one.

"I saw Jesus in his face the first time I ever met him. I was twelve years old, but I've loved him ever since," wrote another.

As a visitor, however, his presence could occasionally be disturbing. He was having supper in a home to which he was a stranger, when one of the young daughters began to criticize and sneer at some godly old evangelist; another member of the house made some withering remark about another body of believers, and Mr. St. John turned quietly to his host, and rising from the table he said, "You won't mind if I go now, will you?" "But," said his host in surprise, "we're only just starting supper!" "Well," replied Mr. St. John, "I've made it a rule never to sit in the company of people who are speaking disparagingly of God's servants. I must ask you either to excuse me or to change the subject."

The subject was changed and the meal proceeded, but next morning when the family had gone off the hostess sought out Mr. St. John and burst into tears. "I couldn't sleep last night," she said, "for thinking of what happened. We've got into the habit of criticizing other Christians, and my boys have grown up to despise preachers. Neither of them was at the meeting last night; if only we could start again and have things different!"

In the countries where he traveled he was often urged to settle and at one time he was on the brink of accepting the head-ship of a large Bible college in America. But it was not to be, and he remained a traveler to the end. Much of the richness of his illustrations sprang from his travels, for wherever he went by sea or land, from mountain scenery, from animal life, from architecture or history, from plant customs or from conversations with children, he gathered material that threw new light on his Bible teaching. In vivid, dramatic language he would relate an experience that would engrave some deep truth indelibly on the mind: how vividly, for instance, he pressed home the doctrine of the heavenly places in the following anecdote!

"A few years ago I was in a zoo in Australia, where they have a magnificent pair of golden eagles, fourteen feet across from the tip of one wing to the tip of the other, and with an unconscious piece of sarcasm they said that these eagles were caged in spacious cages. I stood outside and looked; the cages were about thirty by twenty feet. The catalog might think it a spacious cage, but I should like to have asked the eagles what they thought about a cage where they could just hop backwards and forwards when they were used to soaring towards the sun, mile after mile in limitless space. How many of the Lord's dear people are living in small cages, when they might be soaring to unimagined heights of fellowship with God."

And all the secret of a life hid with Christ in God was flashed upon him, as he crossed a bridge on horseback in South America.

"How does the hidden life manifest itself? I remember years ago in Brazil we had to cross a single plank bridge to reach the main road. Now on this side of the stream there was very seldom sunshine, and the ground was barren and bare; but on the brink of the further shore of the stream there was perpetual sunshine, bright flowers and bushes. One morning as I was going out and just putting my foot on the plank to cross, I noticed on the left hand of the streamlet a magnificent plant in full vigor and beauty. I turned back to see how it was that in this barren and sunless stretch, with circumstances so unfriendly that nothing could really thrive, such a lovely thing had grown, and I was delighted to notice that the plant had come from the other side of the river on which the sun shone. It had sent a tendril that had gripped the grooves of the plank, and then by waving itself about in the air it had found a piece of ground into which it could dig and bury its tendrils, and then a few inches away it had lifted its crest and brought forth exquisite flowers out of the midst of barrenness. It ran from the root for about ten feet, and as it lifted its head you could see that it drew its nourishment from the other side; its life was sustained by the sun shining on the farther shores of the river. And with deep precision I may say that there exactly is the Christian pathway—life in the midst of an unfriendly world, where sin and the gloom of our surroundings might well condemn us to sterility. Yet here and there you will see a man filled with the Spirit, you will see a woman bringing forth fruit to God, and when you meet such people on these unfriendly shores, you wonder how they sustain their lives. This is the hidden life: you died; that is, you cut the links with sin in the past, and your life is hid with Christ—it's up there in the Land of Sunshine; He is your life, and

HAROLD ST. JOHN (standing) and E. H. Broadbent

HAROLD ST. JOHN (right) and W. H. Knox

because you draw from hidden springs, bud, blossom and fruit will be produced."

The Swiss chamois leaping from one pin-point of rock to the other, silhouetted against the sky, lit up the book of Habakkuk; the high snows of the Andes and the tropical forests spoke to him of the climates of the soul. "Whatever the temperature of the soul today, there are the hills of the everlasting God and you may tread them, but to do so you must have hind's feet."

An incident in Australia illustrated the principle of overcoming evil with good. "Just where I was staying," he related, "was a small but very go-ahead town; they built fine buildings, but the citizens were grieved that they had no river. They weren't going to lie under a reproach like that for long, so they dug channels and soon they had a fine river running through the city; but they soon discovered that there was something wrong with the river: the bed was covered with a deadly weed and they dredged it, but it was no good—the weeds came up again; nothing could kill them. Then a wise man came along and said, 'You're wasting your time. All you need to do is to plant a row of poplar trees on either bank and they will take all the goodness of the soil and the weeds will die.' This they actually did; and not only had they conquered the evil, but they had so conquered it by good that they had two fine rows of trees as the result of their difficulties. So don't only get rid of the weeds, but make a festive avenue of green through your struggles."

The broad beam of light from the huge vessel, the *Berengaria,* that guided the pilot ship back to port across the stormy waters of the dark harbor was to him the light of the Word of God. "Wherewith shall youth make its way radiant?" (Psalm 119:9). The only thing those sailors had to do was to bend their backs and row, and follow that track of light across the darkness, until they reached their desired haven. The moment they left the path of light anything might happen.

The roof of Michelangelo's Cistine Chapel in Rome reflected in a mirror placed at a certain angle, spoke to him of the glory of God revealed in Christ. The steadfast set of the compass on a ship tossed far out of its course yet straining to regain its bearings in the storm, reminded him of Christ the steadfast pattern, ever pointing Godwards.

Shattered and battered the ship may be but, as long as it keeps veering round toward the compass, it will reach port.

And in this life of constant travel and change, did he never tire? He certainly did, but he had his own resources. He tells of how once, coming down Broadway, New York, on a hot day, he looked up at the huge sky-scrapers, scores of storeys high, and felt very tired indeed. Then he saw just behind him the little old wooden church where George Washington used to worship, next door to the twenty-five million dollar State Building; so he went into the little church and sat down for a few moments' quiet, and as he sat there the choir boys began singing from the back of the church, "Jesus, Lover of my soul, let me to Thy bosom fly."

"I jumped up," said Mr. St. John; "I was not tired any more. I said, 'Lord, I've found something bigger than the sky scrapers and the banks, and bigger than all the show and flaunting of the wealthiest city in the world. The thing for which this little wooden church stands will last and out live all that!' And I went down Broadway singing the Lord's song. And to my ears the Lord's song never sounded better than when I sang it in Broadway, New York."

As a young man he traveled much with Dr. Alfred Burton in Ireland and with Lord Radstock on the Continent; later with Mr. Payne in S. America and with Mr. Broadbent, Mr. McNair in Brazil and with Mr. Knox and Mr. C. F. Hogg in the USA. But for the most part he traveled alone.

CHAPTER 10

The Churchman

TEN days before his death, Mr. St. John asked for pen and paper, and wrote out his final summing up of the church principles which he had striven to uphold most of his life. It is the labored effort of a dying man, traced out in almost illegible writing, but it was a last urgent plea against narrowness, intolerance and self-righteousness, which things he considered the death-sentence of any true church.

> May 1st, '57: What has religion meant to me?
> 1. Sixty-three years of intimacy with God as revealed in Jesus Christ.
> 2. Sixty-three years of happy church fellowship within the circles of Christians known as 'brethren,' never recognizing any difference of doctrine of any importance between 'open' or 'exclusive,' but with many a glad, gay excursion out into wider circles, always finding the one Book, the same Lord, the same groping for outward unity, the same assurance of one life and nature in the one Spirit and the one Son leading to one Father.
> 3. I accept beloved Mr. Darby's evening counsel to his brethren: 'Remember that you're nothing and nobody except Christians, and on the day you cease to provide an available mount of communion for every recognized believer in the Lord Jesus, you will become sectarian, and merely add, by your meetings, to the disorder and ruin of Christendom.'
> 4. I have followed the guidance of one Book, grateful that millions of fellow-travelers are moving toward the same goal from separate sides of the hill, clutching the same dear Volume. I have sought to walk, as far as loyalty permits, with all Christians, to enjoy as widely as possible Christian fellowship with all.
> 5. Since the New Testament merely gives illustrations and tells us what first century believers did, usually leaving its readers to form judgments for themselves, there must be great breadth of charity and wide divergence in local churches. These differences may exist without any breach of fellowship; there is no fixed pattern of church fellowship, or church order laid down in the Book, beyond:

   a. The rule of elders—Titus 1:5.

   b. The guidance of the Spirit, prominent in times of spiritual freedom and wisdom, but controlled in days of lessened spirituality. See the Pastoral Epistles—Romans, etc.

   c. Because of the fluidity of church order, due to such various levels of power, most that we call church truth must be uncertain, not couched in command, but based on the local members' knowledge and care for one another.

Of ecstasies I have had one or two experiences, only of interest to myself—and of these I am no more certain than St. Paul (2 Cor. 12). The manifestation of John 14:21 stands in a different class, and is the reward of mutual desire and divine service.

I have desired my Lord and He has longed after me.

The tired hand fails here, and the writing trails off, but he had stated the creed and the spirit that he had so earnestly sought to impart to the body of Christians with which he had linked himself.

As a young man he had been brought up, and exercised his early ministry, in a circle of Exclusive Meetings, often called after one of its leaders, Mr. W. J. Lowe, but through contact with all kinds of missionaries abroad he gradually moved into a more open position. In later years the emphasis he placed upon tolerance and broad charity became more and more pronounced, and his own loving appreciation of the work of other groups and the desire for fellowship with all who loved Christ were the foremost legacy he longed to leave with his particular denomination. His emphasis on the need for liberty of conscience and tolerance was perhaps inherited from his ancestor, Oliver Beauchamp St. John, who won the case for the seven bishops against the Crown in the reign of James II. He loved to lead his hearers back to the days before sectarianism existed, to remind them that "the early church was very simple; all the medicine was in the bottle, but there were no labels: for instance, there were Christians in Rome, but no Romanists; men believed in bishops, but there were no Episcopalians; there was lay preaching, but no Methodists; many held the truth as to baptism, but there were no Baptists; men trembled at the Word of God, but there were no Quakers; the Church was an army of salvation, but there was no Salvation Army; Christian hearts were enlarged to one another, but there were no Open Brethren; there were those who were very careful to preserve the holiness of God's House, but there were no Exclusive Brethren. In short, the saints gathered to the Name of the Lord Jesus, but no-one dared to use a name of a sectarian nature. They had the goods without the labels."

That it was right to receive into communion all who loved Christ and acknowledged His Deity was a conviction for which he fought, and for which, towards the end of his life, he suffered. He did not oppose letters of commendation, but he did not really consider that they should be necessary.

"In the first century there were cases when it was well that a traveler should carry a letter—see John's two epistles. The following comes to mind—Barnabas, Saul, Judas and Silas, accredited as chief men among the brethren, and charged with a great service (Acts 15). Apollos had preached a cramped gospel, but had received an access of light, and wishing to spread that light in Greece, he was encouraged by his brethren who wrote to the brethren in that land commending him to their loving care. Phoebe, a business woman, has to visit Rome, and Paul is delighted to give her a letter advising the brethren how they can best serve her interests. The Corinthian elders must write, giving the names and stating their approval of those who are to carry the relief funds to Jerusalem. Timothy is to be welcomed as Paul's fellow-laborer. Mark has a shadow on his reputation and Paul's tender heart would remove it. Titus and his two friends must be shown the proof of love (2 Corinthians 8:16-24). But in all the above cases the reason for giving the letter was to make it easy for those to whom it was addressed to help the bearer. I prefer to draw the veil of silence over the twentieth century letter, which appears to be offered as evidence that So-and-so is in the habit of attending a certain place of worship and has brought a ticket of admission entitling him to a seat and to a share in a loaf and a cup of wine. In the first century any brother with spiritual discernment could tell at once whether a visitor was a member of a body of Christians or not.

"As to reception, the New Testament is clear. Romans 14:1 to 15:7 covers every possible case. We are to receive all who can offer credible evidence that they have owned Jesus Christ as Lord, are discontented with the world and are satisfied with Christ. We gladly extend a loving welcome to all such, and the less formal we are, the better. I recall one simple case: some of you may remember the late Mr. T. H. Reynolds of Burford; he loved to tell how he came into fellowship. He was eight years old and was taken to the Breaking of Bread by his aunt. As they sang 'When I survey the wondrous Cross' she noticed that the child's eyes filled with tears. Later, as the bread was being passed round, he touched his aunt and whispered, 'May I?' She was about to shake her head when a quiet voice said to her, 'Whosoever shall stumble one of these little ones that believe in Me' . . . and she nodded assent. Little Thomas took his place that morning, and ninety years later he passed into the presence of the Lord he had remembered so long.

"I travel about a good deal, and I go to companies of Christians and I sometimes find they're all very much taken up with the question as to who should be allowed to walk in Christian fellowship with them. These things may sometimes be necessary, but it is never a compliment to the spiritual side of a church when they have to discuss who is worthy to break bread with them. I will tell you why not. Because the early church never had a reception question at all. You read in Acts 5:13, 'Of the rest dared no man join himself to them.' Why not? Because the Christians at that time were so conspicuously holy that nobody except those who were right with God and anxious to be holy too would ever dream of coming within forty feet of them.

"The assembly of God's people has a three-fold stand: Is it catholic? Is it scriptural? Is it holy? Take the first of these three words: 'catholic,' a magnificent word! I know it has been filched and made the property of a large sect; it has been utterly smirched and defiled, but the word simply means 'universal.' That is, the assembly of God embraces, in its function and spiritual desire, every member of the Body of Christ. Anything less than that is essentially sectarian. The apostle writes, 'To the church of God which is at Corinth, with all that in every place call upon the Name of Jesus Christ our Lord, both theirs and ours.' That is, plainly the first thought of the church is that she is necessarily catholic. You may have twenty different banners flying in the district; see to it that you yourselves, whatever your views on Christendom, are nothing and nobody but Christians, and that your assembly provides for, and welcomes, every consistent Christian who seeks to walk with you in the neighborhood."

He loved to look back to the origins of the great denominations and claim his own share in the doctrines for which their founders lived and died. He maintained that the great blunder of the Corinthian church and the cause of all their party spirit was that they said, "I belong to Paul, or Apollos," instead of, "Paul belongs to us." "They were putting the cart before the horse," said Mr. St. John. "They didn't belong to Paul; Paul belonged to them. If we understood that, all the sectarianism in the church would disappear tomorrow. You would not say, 'I belong to Wesley,' nor 'I belong to Martin Luther,' but 'He belongs to me.' Look at chapter 3—'All things are yours, whether Paul, or Apollos, or Cephas—all are yours.' What did he mean? He means that all the great spiritual men and ministers of the past belong to us, every one. I have a share in St. Augustine, Martin Luther, John Bunyan, C. H. Spurgeon. Every one belongs to me, but I belong to none of them. In certain small sects the leaders warn their adherents not to read books written by people who belong to other circles. Why do they do that? Because they know that the moment their adherents begin to range in the fields of Spirit-given ministry, they will find out how very little they have got."

Yet although he battled against sectarianism and emphasis on non-essential details, he was also careful to guard the fellowship of those who loved Christ, and he illustrated this by a masterly exposition on the City of God in Revelation 21. "You must be careful—that is why there is a wall, great and high. You must not let the grievous wolves come in; you must keep all the safeguards of sanctity. But when you have built the wall and are sure that it is high enough, then you must pierce the wall with twelve gates. That means you want to welcome into your hearts and affections every person who loves the Lord. First your walls, then your gates."

Who, then, would he exclude from church fellowship? No-one on the grounds that they usually walked with another denomination, but anyone who by doctrine or by life was openly dishonoring the Lord. "The table proclaims and asserts the one-ness of the Body of Christ, and therefore every person whom you can confidently recognize as having an interest in the death of Christ, every person who shares in that precious blood, has a divine and inalienable right to take his place at the Supper of the Lord. If you should ask me on what grounds you should refuse a person, I would say at once that there are only three reasons in the New Testament:

"Firstly, doctrine of such a character that you cannot recognize the man to be a Christian at all—the man who does not believe that Jesus is very God, or who does not believe that the Scriptures are a divine revelation. Secondly, practice—a man who is an evil liver (and do remember what is called a wicked person in 1 Corinthians 5 includes a covetous man and a man who speaks evil against his brethren)—'Put away from yourselves that wicked person.' Sometimes I wonder whether church discipline is not a deal too narrow. Listen to the Scripture—'Put away from yourselves that wicked person'—yes, a covetous man or a man who speaks evil against his brethren; the Scripture tells us that he is to be in isolation, for such a one is deadly sick in his soul. Thirdly, if a man comes from a place where the name of the Lord Jesus and the Bible are dishonored and he asserts his claim as a Christian, I would hesitate to say, 'Yes;' for the apostle John says, 'If there comes a man into your midst not bringing the doctrine of Christ, you are to refuse him admittance.' That is, we are to recognize with open-eyed clearness every person who desires fellowship with us. As a sharer in the love of Christ his doctrine must be clear, his life must be clean, and his associations must not compromise the foundations upon which the Christian Church rests."

But, to him, foundations meant the foundations laid by Christ and the apostles, never the differing superstructures that man throughout the centuries has erected upon them. In these he recognized necessary and Spirit-guided variations. "Church life should draw from two sources," he maintained. "First the written Scripture, sovereign as far as it was spoken; secondly the living Spirit, ruling, guiding and enabling the local church to function and to face the changing conditions of each age. Darby has some excellent remarks as to the carnality of those who demand a text for every detail of church life. If we accepted such a false principle, our hymn books, our Sunday Schools, our printed Bibles would all have to go overboard. The New Testament churches all met in private houses, hence the phrase 'the church in thy house.'"

Mr. St. John recognized certain essentials laid down in the Scriptures, and these only he considered fundamental and basic to all worship, although the Spirit might lead in certain cases to add to them. "The traveling furniture of the pilgrim Church is exceedingly simple," he once said. "There are four things you cannot do without. You must have a pool, a loaf of bread, a flagon of wine and a Book. And all that the Church needs for carrying on her ritual service in the way of outward observance are these four things—the water, the bread, the cup and the Book.

"In the Acts of Paul we find a permanent pattern of church life. The authority was vested in a local assembly in which was appointed a body of elders, or a presbytery (Acts 14:23, 20:17, Titus 1:5). In Philippians 1:1 we find named in a single verse the three constituent elements of the New Testament church: saints who lead beautiful lives, bishops (or elders) who rule, deacons who serve.

"Elsewhere we read of the young men who buried Ananias, evangelists, attendants like John Mark, leading men among the brethren (Acts 15:22, Hebrews 13:7, 17, 24). The service of Christian women is widely dealt with (1 Cor. 11:4-5 and 14:34-35) and there were deaconesses. For a special emergency Paul was perfectly willing to appoint a body of seven collectors for a famine relief fund (Acts 20:4, 1 Cor. 16:1-4)."

He laid great emphasis on the fact that every man and every woman had their contribution to make in church life, and that the old should be constantly preparing the young for future leadership and responsibility. "We read that our young men are to be as plants, grown up in their youth," he said, "and the Bible makes a great deal of the way things are handed on from generation to generation. Jacob called his twelve sons when dying. Moses does the same in his full vigor; he says to Joshua: 'These are the things God has taught me. Take them, carry them through life, and do not lose any precious thing handed down to you.'

"Do you younger men understand that you are the heirs of one of the most remarkable phases in the Church's history? God has been bringing out light as to the assembly, truth as to the Holy Spirit, clearer thoughts as to the person of Christ, and the gospel is being preached with a fullness and clearness our grandfathers never knew. You have become the heirs of a great deposit of precious truth. How are you going to use the testimony placed in your hands? If Christ tarries, you will soon be leaders and fathers of the assemblies. Where are you going to lead the sheep? Are you by constant fellowship with God preparing yourself for the tremendous task before you in coming years? I know that means that we older men must not do everything. The Levites of fifty years of age laid aside their service and put it into the hands of younger men, and as a man gets older he should pass on much to the younger men.

"I do like our sons in the assemblies to be like plants growing up in their youth (Psa. 144:12), but the most important part of the growing plant is out of sight. Young man, remember that. It is not your presence at the Prayer Meeting, admirable and necessary as that is, nor even at the Lord's Supper nor at the Sunday School, that shows the real inner heart of your Christian life. Everything depends on your life in your closed room, your study of your Bible and your prayer life.

"The second point is that our daughters may be as cornerstones, polished after the similitude of a palace. The significance of these two symbols is, first, dependability and trustworthiness, and then moral and spiritual beauty. In the older days of the Tabernacle, the men carried the heavy boards and the women did the spinning and drawing of the threads tightly; and unless the curtains had been well spun, there would have been no Tabernacle at all. The work of the women was to pull the threads together, keep things uniform and connected; and when Moses talks of the loops he calls them 'sisters,' and it is to the sisters as a class that the unity of the church is entrusted. When a meeting is going on happily I always want to ask, 'Where are the sisters?' For God has put the moulding of the lives of your husbands, lovers, brothers and sons into your hands—the moulding of their characters, manners, and so on. So remember you are called to be absolutely dependable in every crisis, and as beautiful in character as the shining walls of a palace. The strength of the assembly is in the hands of the brethren, the beauty and unity in the hands of the sisters."

There was room and ministry for all, and he loved to urge every member of the local church to discover his own niche. He often illustrated the point by the following anecdote:

"I had a delightful experience in Devonshire some time ago. A good man asked me to tea and began to tell me his experiences over the tea-table. He told me, 'For about twenty years I was possessed with the idea that I was meant to preach, but I always found a queue of others who wanted to do the same thing. I never found that anyone urged me to do so, except my wife; but after many years of this sort of thing I decided that I'd been making a mistake, and there were other services to be done. I had a little money, and I went round and began to visit poor Christians. I took the old ladies a pound of tea and other little things to meet their need, and I was so encouraged with this that I bought a bath chair, and I used to go round and fetch Mrs. A. to the meeting and sit her in her seat, and then run back and fetch Mr. B. Thus I used to bring along two or three and it was a delight to my soul; and do you know, I never found a queue of brethren waiting to go up to the cottages and visit the sick, nor a queue of bath chairs at the door of anyone's cottage!' He had found his niche. He had ceased to burden the church with his empty ministry, but every effort and mile with that bath chair are, I believe, written in the books of heaven."

Truth, charity, humility, and clear, consistent witness were to him the marks of the true church, and he deplored the time and energy spent on trivial, unimportant details. "There's a tendency in us, as we grow older," he warned his hearers, "to become very busy with external things. We are enormously interested in who can come into our meetings, what bread and wine we should use, whether we should have an organ. I could tell you twenty or thirty things that fill men's minds to the exclusion of large, good things. But men like that live in the suburbs. They just play about with the scaffolding of church life, and, says Paul with tremendous dignity, remember the Christian has died with Christ to all that sort of thing. The function of the church is a big thing. As the late Lord Salisbury used to say, 'Gentlemen, for the love of God let us buy big maps.' Look at things largely and don't spend your life playing with pieces of scaffolding. Do we understand that the task and business of the Church is that she is the army of Jehovah, fighting massed forces of Satan, sin and death? And all these petty little things that divide the heart of the saints is merely giving ammunition to the hosts of evil and weakening the spiritual power of saints. We are not here to play at churches. Lots of men frequently do that. Some article of church furniture fills their attention and thought for months, or they are tremendously concerned as to whether they should recognize another group of Christians. Are we playing at churches, or are we building churches? Here we are in a dark world, and Christ has given us a tremendous task of letting the light of the Scriptures shine out. Here we are in a starving world, and our supreme business is to feed the flock. But we chatter like sparrows about unimportant detail. Oh the pity, the pity!"

But the heart of all Harold St. John's church life, and the crowning hour of the week, was the Breaking of Bread. If possible, he would start out an hour or two early on Sunday morning to spend time alone, sometimes arriving in a state of such high adoration as to be scarcely conscious of his surroundings. One day he reached the Hall about twenty minutes early and sat down, absorbed. Suddenly he rose to his feet, an unearthly light upon his face, and went forward to the table to break the bread, only just realizing in time that the service had not yet started. Many remember him more clearly at the Communion Table than anywhere else. The lifted face, the solemn sense of holiness, the almost dumb amazement giving way to a soaring expression of adoration, and the richness and beauty of his ministry. The action week by week colored his whole life. It was a pledge of loyalty and service, the renewing of a covenant week by week. "The man in whose hand the cup is found, he shall be my servant" was a verse he loved to reiterate.

For forty years he hardly missed the Sunday morning Breaking of Bread in some form or other, and when he was bedridden the bread and wine were carried to his bedside. At the end of his life he yearned to gather once more with others round the Lord's Table, and his wish was granted. The service was held in the house where he lay rapidly failing, and he was carried down in a wheeled chair. It was Easter Sunday, three weeks before he died. Later on in the day he was heard murmuring, "Now lettest Thou Thy servant depart in peace, for my eyes have seen Thy salvation."

"In any case, I love Him," he once said, summing up the meaning of the sacrament; "so I do what He says; I remember Him. The Father delights in Christ's death, so I show it to high heaven. I place a horizon on my thinking: He's coming back, so I will do it until He comes. If I did not believe that the Lord Jesus Christ was coming back, and that I would see Him, I would never break bread again in my life."

It is impossible to gauge the extent of his influence on the assemblies of those with whom he worshiped, but at least it is safe to say that wherever he preached on these aspects of church life, men's hearts were enlarged with a wider charity, and their eyes were lifted above pettiness and narrowness, to look at least for a moment at the vision of the Church, redeemed, united, militant, called unto holiness, terrible as an army with banners. And maybe they shared a little of Mr. St. John's own sorrow that the reality was often so far from the ideal.

"If we are satisfied with our church life," he once wrote, "may God have pity on us and blast it, that we may wake up to life's realities. If we are not satisfied, let us afflict ourselves before God and seek a right way for us, for our little ones, and for all our substance (Ezra 8:21)."

CHAPTER 11

The Bible Student

MEN who shared the platform with Mr. St. John were always amazed at his accurate knowledge of the Book to whose study he devoted a large part of his life. Professor F. F. Bruce writes: "We younger men referred to him as 'The Maestro,' but not to his face, as he would have strongly deprecated any attempt to place him on a higher level than those who delighted to sit at his feet. For detailed acquaintance with the text of Scripture he had few equals."

Mr. G. C. D. Howley comments: "His command of Scripture was seen to full advantage when he was leading a conversational Bible Reading and answering questions. His answers were always immediate, and he would give full measure, pressed down and running over, full and informative beyond the expectation of his hearers." It was his truly amazing knowledge and the insight into Holy Scripture that caused the late Mr. Fred Mitchell, Home Director of the China Inland Mission, to describe him as "the man who knew his Bible better than anyone else in Britain." From all parts of the Bible he drew his material and his answers to questions. A classic example is of his being asked for an explanation of the words in Hebrews 9:22, "Almost all things are by the law purged with blood." He replied immediately that there were half a dozen exceptions, and quoted a list of six instances where blood was not required for purification. On another occasion the lights went out during a large meeting while he was reading a rather obscure passage. While the lighting was being attended to, Mr. St. John went quietly on, reciting the passage from memory.

There was a legend, probably not far from the truth, that he could give the reference for every verse in the Bible; and the children he knew best when he lived at Clarendon School in later years used to love to shoot unexpected texts at him. But they seldom, if ever, succeeded in catching him out, not even the small, golden-haired girl who fixed him with a diminutive forefinger and stated solemnly, "Thy wife shall be a harlot in the city," and Mr. St. John replied with equal solemnity, "Amos 7:17," after which both relapsed into a state of mutual admiration and glee; for Mr. St. John had a great weakness for small, golden-haired girls.

But the knowledge was hard won. "Here we come to this dear Book that we've learned to love as light," he once said as he opened a meeting; but that love was the result of countless hours of patient study, self-tuition in Greek and Hebrew, and exhaustive exploration along every channel that might throw new light on some word or verse. One wrote of him, "Behind his outstanding facility of speech was an industry that explains it, though this was so far-reaching that few could grasp it fully. We have in our possession some of his working books, in which every Hebrew or Greek word used in the book he was studying at the time is listed. There would follow separate lists, giving every reference to certain main themes in the book, the leading ideas, and sometimes the minor points also, set out in the same careful detail; the divine names, etc., etc., so that each working book so filled represented the most indefatigable workmanship. Nothing was left to chance or feeling, and his knowledge of Scripture was based upon the most thorough research. We have met him in London sometimes and found him busy at work with technical books beside him, and always his Revised Version Bible at his hand. His reading was wide, and he was versed in the writing of most schools of thought, besides having somehow fitted in the reading of many of the really important contemporary expository or theological works."

These notes filled thousands of loose-leaved sheets and represented the passion of his life. "Many a night in my youth," he once told his young hearers, "(though God forbid you should be so foolish) the blaze of the light of Scripture has so grown upon me that I have seen light breaking in the dawn before I could tear myself away from my Bible as the Book poured its treasures out. Many a time long hours have passed chasing one word to its lair, one tense to its perfection. And remember this, man's life will never be lonely, never be broken, never be wearisome, if he makes friends with Moses and the prophets, and, supremely, with Christ."

HAROLD ST. JOHN and W. E. VINE searching the Scriptures

One thing that specially struck Professor Bruce was the way he never reverted to old study. "To the end of his days," wrote the Professor, "he imposed on himself the discipline of study, and that was one reason for the perennial freshness of his ministry. The gold which he brought forth from the Divine Treasury was always fresh minted." In his closing years, when he taught Scripture to the girls at Clarendon School, he prepared his lessons with as much conscientious thoroughness as if he were digesting them for the first time. Late in life, when giving a series of lectures on a certain book of the Bible at South Park Chapel, Ilford (perhaps the place where he felt more at home than any other), he confessed to having read through the book in question a hundred times previously.

"Let my younger brethren remember," he warned them, "that true ministry must rest upon a platform of knowledge only acquired by holy, constant meditation in the Word of God. Kept manna breeds worms. A man who meditates in the Law day and night will always be fresh and thoughtful in his teaching of Christ."

Like David he could have said, "Oh, how I love Thy Law!" "I have been fifty years a Christian," he once remarked. "I've never suffered five minutes' boredom in all those years. Every new morning sees something fresh to study." And indeed he would come out from his room in the early morning, his face radiant like the face of a man who has seen God's glory. Often the lingering joy of that communion was so great that he must find someone with whom to share it, and would seek out some other member of the family and greet them with, "I've had such a wonderful time with the Lord this morning!" Then he would sit down beside them and eagerly point out the verse or passage in question with the suppressed excitement of one who has made some great new discovery.

In one of his editorial articles in *The Bible Scholar* he explained something of the place that the Bible held in his heart as he saw it in the whole Christian system. The following is an extract from part of the article:

> This morning I was reading a compressed report of a conversation between a priest of the Roman Church and an aged Christian named Angelica, who lives in one of the villages of Umbria, in Italy.

She was sitting outside her cottage, reading her Bible, when a passing priest addressed her:

Priest: What is that that you are reading?
Angelica: The Word of God, Sir.
Priest: How do you know it's God's Word?
Angelica: (Pointing to the sky) What is that light in the sky?
Priest: Why, the sun of course.
Angelica: How does your Reverence know that it's the sun?
Priest: Because it gives me light and warmth.
Angelica: I thank you, Sir. That's exactly how I know that this Book is God's Word. It gives me light and warmth also.

This neatly worded retort will serve to introduce what I wish to write about, namely, the central place held by Holy Scripture in the Christian system.

I wonder how many of my readers ever sat down and considered what would be the moral and intellectual condition of civilization if the Bible was blotted out from our mental sky; if, after all, it could be shown that our faith was only beautiful myth? In the main, our loss would be threefold: firstly, we should be robbed of the only revelation of God which we possess. It is almost universally admitted that there is no serious rival to the Bible in our days. Scholars have examined the classics of the ancient world and the sacred books of the East, and by men outside and inside the Church they are confessed to be spiritually sterile. The Word of God has spanned the arch of history, and has withstood the shocks and discoveries of centuries. If this Word could fail us, our only idea of God would be that of a kind of super-millionaire, living far away across the Ocean of Eternity, and leaving his starving family to perish upon an unfriendly shore, refusing to send even one gleam of light to mitigate the darkness, or one crumb of bread to satisfy their hunger.

Again, our only fixed standard of morals would have fallen. If we surrender the Scripture, we lose the eternal difference between right and wrong, and every man and nation becomes a law unto itself—Politics and religion can both become merely the manifestations of man's unfettered spirit, and we sink slowly into the morass beneath our own corruption.

Thirdly, our only hope of salvation is extinguished. Our racial history records an age-long warfare between sin and righteousness; in our dealings with vice and crime we swing between the iron severity of the laws of Draco, the tyrant of Athens, and the soft comfort of the modern penitentiary. Our statesmen feverishly explore every available avenue in search of a specific for our disease, and hope that by better methods of education we shall reach social salvation; but meanwhile the problems of human sin and sorrow stare at us like a row of skulls.

The Bible and the Bible alone holds out to us a final solution for our perplexities. It tells us of a pierced hand strong enough to lift the lowest from his degradation; of wounded feet fleet enough to follow the most wayward feet; and it reveals to us the cleansing stream that flowed from the Cross.

Mr. St. John has been called a man of one Book, but, as has been mentioned, he read widely round his subject. In fact, the range and variety of his reading were amazing, but it was all directed towards the ultimate goal of a better understanding and truer exposition of the Bible. He liked to keep abreast of the broad trend of history and politics, and particularly science: "For a Christian, science is merely the unravelling of the fringe of the Lord's garment," he wrote in a letter to a younger man. "Discoveries teach us the materials of which His robes are made; they will lead me to deeper trust in Him, not to doubt His existence." Yet occasionally he could wax ironical on the subject. "It is now generally believed," he once said, "that the world will ultimately be destroyed by fire. Strangely enough, a fisherman told us that two thousand years ago; but he didn't know any science!"

Yet he was strangely uninterested in controversy, and was so loth to press his own views on the ordinary controversial subjects on which orthodox Christians differ, that he was sometimes suspected as not having any. Those who thought this were quite mistaken. His personal attitude to the Second Advent, for instance, is clearly indicated by these words: "I know that for myself I love to draw up the blinds in the morning and say, 'It may be today,' and pull them down at night thinking, 'Perhaps before dawn,' but I shall be told by men of far deeper spirituality than myself that I'm wrong in this. It matters little. I have not found that divergence in prophetic views dims the eye of faith or hinders a life in the gladness of God."

He was often, during the last war, asked his views on noncombatism, and he realized that in some assemblies it was becoming a real bone of contention. Certain opening remarks of a talk he gave on the subject, while leaving every man free to follow the dictates of his conscience, brought both parties more or less into line and unity before the question was ever even faced in detail.

"The results of this brief enquiry may be this: you will be in a better position for clear thinking; not necessarily to agree with your brethren, but to see that instead of your sitting on the top of the North Pole and your brother freezing on top of the South Pole, there may possibly be some temperate clime for you both. And the first thing we need to do is to define our terms. I understand that a militarist is a man who delights wholeheartedly in war; but in all the men and women I know there isn't one militarist—we are all pacifists in that we hate and dread the shadow of war falling on our shores and our homes. The only point in which Christians differ is as to the best means to gain the goal of peace toward which all our faces are set. And this to begin with might perhaps bring us a little nearer, make our faces a little less red and the veins stand out less pronouncedly upon our necks when we discuss these matters."

For he was a man of far horizons. Seen against the whole, wide perspective of Biblical truth, the controversy in itself often appeared a mere unimportant detail, a matter of opinion, while the atmosphere of ill-will and emotion and heat that it might provoke could cloud the whole of a man's spiritual life. He had no room for real heresy, but he was slow to apply the term to the convictions of an honest Christian. "The term 'heresy' might be applied to such movements as Christian Science," he affirmed, "provided the speaker were in a very humble frame of mind."

"The letter killeth, but the spirit giveth life," and in all Mr St. John's studies he was searching for two things—never for mere knowledge but, firstly, for a fresh, fairer view of Christ. Knowledge that stops short of this becomes an end in itself, he said, a dangerous stumbling block to any age. To an old friend, Mr. Robert Balloch, he wrote, "We who are constantly thinking of the Scriptures are in danger of becoming mere channels of information from the Book to its hearers. May you and I be kept in simplicity, more engaged with Christ than with sermons or readings."

And to a group of young people he uttered this solemn warning with regard to their study: "It is not enough for us to be living in the Book, blessed and holy as that Book is. It is always possible to be greatly engaged with the text of Holy Scripture, and even to be considering its meaning, without ever really reaching Christ. So remember, the Bible is never the end in itself. It is not the home of the heart, but it's the official highway that leads to it. It's the path by which you reach Christ, and it is that which tells you all you know of Him historically. But tell me, is that all you want? Will a historical Christ satisfy you? Do you want simply to know facts about Him, or to keep company with Christ, to have Him show things to your heart that are in the Bible, but which come fresh from Him to you?

"There is no man in this building who gives more reverence, more honor, more love to this Book than I. But I'm sure that even in the use of it there's a danger lest we should stop short of reaching the One to whom this Book bears witness. If your mind's been merely engaged with texts, or you've merely been considering passages out of the Bible, you've lacked something. You haven't gone all the way, for all the way is this: that the Lord Jesus Christ should present Himself to you as the only safe Guide on the dangerous road of life and the only way by which you can keep your pathway shining; that is, that the face of Christ should shine upon you, and you should behold as in a mirror the glory of the Lord. The Word, yes; but not the Word only, always the Word with the Spirit. There are scholars who have devoted forty years to the most painstaking study of every preposition and word in the Old Testament, but some of them are still a million leagues away from Christ. But remember, this is the problem: how can youth keep its way shining through a dark world? How can you reach the goal—Christ? By taking heed thereto, by stepping carefully and guiding your life by what your soul is learning of God in the text of Holy Scripture, and by keeping company with Christ as your best Friend—never ceasing until you are on such terms with Him that you talk to Him more intimately than to wife or child, lover or friend, and He talks with you. That does not only mean you have a Bible in your pocket—thank God if you have—but it means that you have Christ in your heart."

Secondly, Harold St. John never considered any study really worth while unless it affected one's daily conduct in a practical way. He insisted on this in particular when he studied the prophetic books, where a student may become side-tracked into the pursuit of dispensational truth while neglectful of any immediate practical value. In a series of lectures on the Revelation he emphasized this strongly. "I think this has been a great mistake in the study of dispensational truth: people have taken a passage and found, sometimes with a great deal of ingenuity, that they can fit it into the future, and they are enormously pleased with the discovery. But that never finishes the thing unless you read it again and say, 'Lord, what has this got for me today?' The dispensational interpretation of a passage is never its final meaning. The final meaning is always in the court of conscience. A dispensation is temporal, but you must find the eternal meaning. How does it fit into the realm of the soul? How does it answer some need of the heart?

"For God never places any event in the future without anything that saints can enjoy today. To every saint today, if only he has insight and spirituality enough to receive it, God says, 'You can by faith have everything now that I'm going to give to my saints in the future, and there's not a single blessing in the Millennium that you cannot enjoy by faith today.'"

And how he strove to impress upon the assemblies, where he visited, the need of systematic Bible teaching, book by book, chapter by chapter, and how he mourned the dying out of this practice in many circles. "We are not doing it as our fathers used to do," he said in an urgent appeal towards the close of his life. "I remember in my youth how the late William Kelly used to come up to London and deliver his annual series of lectures. He would take perhaps seven lectures on Isaiah, on the captivity books, and each year he would lecture on some broad portion of Scripture. He spent months preparing his lectures, and there would be queues outside the largest hall they could get, and the good man would speak in a very studied, cultured English for over an hour, simply opening up the Word of God. I spoke to some young people in a meeting to which I came not long ago, because I wanted to know what line to take, and I said, 'When did you last have a series of lectures on the Epistle to the Romans?' They looked surprised and said, 'We've never had such a thing.' And I said, 'When did you last have a series of lectures on the Messianic Psalms or the Song of Solomon?' And they said, 'We've never heard of such a thing.' And I shook my head at those elders and wondered what they'd been up to, not feeding the flock properly. Now we understand that the first thing for which an assembly of God stands is that it be a place where the Scriptures are interpreted as God gave them; that is, by chapters, by books, and by sections, not in text preaching. I do not object to text preaching; I'm only saying it's not the way God gave Scripture; He gave it in big masses, not in texts, and I would say with great deference to my elders, 'I beseech you that you be exercised that you feed the flock of God. On your bookshelves you have books of lectures delivered by God's servants forty years ago, but what is the use of them if you are not having any lectures? And the first thing to expect of an assembly is that it be a place for the exposition of the Word, to declare unto us the parable, open the Bible book by book, chapter by chapter, section by section, till our youth is grounded and settled in the Word of God as He gave it.'"

He himself loved to give series of lectures on some book or topic, and there were certain churches who felt that their spiritual growth was partly due to these lectures. His lectures on church life in Wellington, New Zealand, and his annual Bible Studies at South Park Chapel, Seven Kings, certainly had a profound influence on his hearers. One who heard him year by year at South Park wrote: "He loved to guide his hearers into an intensive study of the books of the Bible; he has given as many as sixteen addresses in a month when expounding some book of the Scriptures; and a careful check of available local records revealed that since the year 1910 most of the books of the Bible received detailed attention."

He sought to inspire every earnest young Christian with this ideal of finding Christ in the Scriptures through painstaking, sanctified study; for he considered it an integral part of the Christian life. He once visited a young Christian university student and examined with pleasure a score of neat notebooks representing months of research in science. After careful examination of these volumes, Mr. St. John said, "Now show me your Bible study books," to which the young man replied with some embarrassment, "I haven't any, Sir, and indeed I shouldn't know how to treat the Bible that way."

The incident stirred Mr. St. John deeply. Here, as he pointed out, was a young man, able to give hours daily to meticulous, accurate study, yet only occasionally flinging a few fag ends of time to the profoundest subject that can engage the human mind—the study of the Book so marvelous that it cost the death of Christ to make its production possible; so powerful that by it alone we can keep ourselves from the power of the destroyer. And in order to help those who wanted to embark on the adventure of Bible Study he twice at least gave examples of his own method of study, taking the two Epistles, Ephesians and Philemon.

When asked as to commentaries and helps to Bible Study, he wrote the following answer:

"A man who deals with Scripture has a conscience which needs to be trained, a heart which must be warmed, and a will that should be yielded, and, finally, a mind which must be fed.

"For the conscience, none is better than Alexander Whyte—his *Lord, Teach Us to Pray* and *With Mercy and with Judgment* will make his readers hot and ashamed. For the heart, *Rutherford's Letters* (not his *Sermons*) and Blaise Pascal's *Thoughts* are invaluable. For the education of the will, the *Confession of St. Augustine* and John Bunyan's *Grace Abounding* are simply unpriced.

"For the more routine departments of the brain, I like to have within reach Dr. Orr's invaluable five volumes, *International Standard Bible Encyclopaedia,* the three volumes of the *Englishman's Greek and Hebrew Concordance,* Andrew Juke's *Types of Genesis,* a model of mystical interpretation (waters to swim in, not for paddlers), Westcott on *John* (English edition) Westcott on *Hebrews,* but, if his Greek hinders, then Davidson's small handbook on Hebrews is most thoughtful. For the Acts Rackham in the *Westminster Commentary* is excellent and full, and, if Stifler's *Acts of the Apostles* is obtainable, it will well repay reading several times.

"The best general commentary is the *Speaker's;* it is old, but very reliable and scholarly. It may be picked up secondhand."

When asked at the very end of his life about the dates of the Epistles, he scribbled his own thoughts on the subject from memory in pencil, but added at the bottom of the list, "Several are only approximate, up to fluctuations of 2-3 years. It matters little, as you simply shift all the figures. Bruce is best. Rackham gets tied up with many monks. Stick to Freddie!"

From the first glow of conversion to almost the last day of life, he never lost his appetite for the study of the Bible, and when he could no longer pass on his findings in public addresses, he said quietly, leaning back in bed with the worn old book in his hand, "It is no longer seed for the sower, but it's wonderful bread for the eater." And it was this bread that moulded his thoughts and character and made him what he was. He once categorized the direct results of Bible Study as follows:

a. The mental horizon widens. It is impossible to live in an intellectual prison if we are in constant contact with this unique library, in which the world's finest poetry, deepest philosophy, and noblest literature abound. In Scripture alone do we discover a lucid, trustworthy account of earth's origin and our own descent; a history of our race, written from the standpoint of its Creator, a final interpretation of the meaning and glory of life; and above all a light, whose rays illumine the far-flung future, enabling us to peer down into the lake of fire as well as to look upwards and count the towers of the city of God. In a sentence, no man can really be called well-educated if he does not know his Bible, nor badly educated if he does.

b. The manners are refined. To breathe the pure air of Holy Writ, to keep company with the holiest and highest of our race, necessarily softens our natural roughness, and we insensibly adopt the court manners of heaven. Some years ago I listened to a brother who while preaching so far forgot himself as to refer to a fellow-servant of Christ in a disparaging way. Later as we walked home together I sensed he was uncomfortable, but I said nothing until he asked me outright what I thought of his performance. 'Well,' I replied, 'I thought you'd been neglecting Paul's Epistles lately.' 'What do you mean?' said he. I answered, 'I don't think that one could be much in the company of such an exquisitely courteous gentleman as the Apostle Paul, without learning not to criticize one's fellow-Christians.'

c. Bible study feeds and fortifies the faith, thus making it sane and robust. We live in a time when fresh, fancy religions flourish like poison fungi. These systems owe their success to the fact that Christians do not know their Bibles, and are easily caught in the toils. It is the absence of fixed beliefs and spiritual landmarks that make men an easy prey to error.

d. But after all, Scripture is only a road. The home of the heart is God, known and loved as Christ knew and loved Him. If we follow the light, it will lead us to our resting place, which perhaps we had forgotten (Jeremiah 50:6). Here is the glory of Bible Study: that if we learn God's will, and then do it, we shall grow like God. But its peril is that we rest content with a knowledge of the text and go no further, like travelers who sit down in the road and imagine they have reached the king's palace.

The Bible became the atmosphere in which he lived and breathed, nor had he any other atmosphere to recommend to those who wanted to grow in grace. "I shall always remember with gratitude your indulgent love to me as a new-born babe in Christ," wrote a young architect. "I shall never forget your last advice as we parted at the head of the main stairs that Easter—never to neglect the daily reading of the Scriptures, and to take time to meditate upon some portion."

And Mr. Eric Hutchings, the well-known evangelist, wrote the following testimony: "Mr. Harold St. John has been one of the greatest spiritual influences of my life. It was he above all others who inspired me to get down to a detailed study of the Bible as the Word of God, to seek the plain and obvious meanings of the words, rather than to attempt to see typical meanings, sometimes abstruse and remote, in everything. By this sane, prayerful approach the true typical teaching of Scripture emerged. In other words, he taught me that it was necessary to go to the Scripture first and let the Word of God unfold itself rather than get hold of some dispensational or typical outline and force the interpretation of such a meaning. He stayed with us in Manchester many times during the years 1935-1945, and even when he was not staying with us, we would lunch together once or twice a week to discuss the things of God. My last meeting with him was typical. He boarded the train at Crewe, at the time when the Billy Graham Crusades were on, and came into the compartment where I was. He talked of the evident working of God through Billy Graham, and his true catholicity of spirit, and burden that all should have the Word of God was once again glowingly evident. It was the last time I saw him. . . his face radiant with the glory of God."

CHAPTER 12

The Man

Some men are only gay in sunny weather,
But my man's joyful rain and shine together.

And some are critical and naught can please,
But my man thinks it perfect if I sneeze!

And others never praise; they fuss and whine,
But everything I do is simply fine!

And some men's appetites are hard to please,
But my man's quite content with bread and cheese.

And if I wrote these couplets by the score,
I could but praise this dear man more and more.

So looking back across the years I can
But say, 'Oh, thank you, God, for such a man,
For, there never was a man like my man.'

*—Extracts from a gay rhyme written by his wife for
their 31st Wedding Anniversary.*

HAROLD St. John carries ten cubic feet of holiness about with him, and you can feel it," wrote one of the leaders of the Young Life Campaign.

"The most saintly man I have ever known closely, of any creed," wrote a member of the Roman church.

"There was an atmosphere of peace and other-worldliness about him which was a very real means of blessing to us," remarked a lady who had sat near him at a dinner table.

"I regarded Mr. St. John as one of the greatest Christians I have ever met. His face was a perfect inspiration, for he just walked with God," wrote a senior missionary in the China Inland Mission.

Yet there was nothing aloof or remote about him, except that he loved solitude. "He radiated joy," wrote a close friend. When in contact with his fellow men there was a warmth and geniality that attracted all types. The Chairman of Netherhall Largs described it as a fragrant, Christ-like courtesy, and another old and valued friend of his, Mr. A. H. Boulton, expressed it as a remarkable loveliness of character, a meekness and gentleness not born of weakness but of spiritual strength and communion with God.

"We always regarded him as a perfect Christian gentleman," wrote another, in whose home he had often stayed. "His gracious, generous spirit has been both a challenge and an inspiration to us. His touching and kindly interest in our children's pleasures was the mark of a great and generous man. His refusal to speak unkindly of any, however much provoked, was a similar mark. Certainly the Holy Spirit had stamped on him in a striking way the features of divine love as seen in 1 Corinthians 13.

"Withal, we loved him for his selflessness. A prince among the saints, he seemed most happy, like his Master, to go among the lowly. Though a man of culture, fine breeding and sensitiveness, we admired that grace which made him prefer to travel steerage or live in a Salvation Army hostel for down-and-outs in order to show them the grace of Christ. Only his Master can rightly evaluate his Nazariteship and the hardships he so joyfully imposed upon himself in his disciplined, self-sacrificing service."

Discipline, humility, courtesy, joy—the words were reiterated hundreds of times over in letters received after his death, as the outstanding marks of Mr. St. John's character. As one pondered them they seemed as linked as the steps of a ladder. The bottom rung a man must lay for himself by a continuous act of will-power and self-denial until self ceases to become important; and out of this proved self-forgetful humility there springs that reverence and regard for others which must always be the fruit of a heart at leisure from itself. And in one that asks for nothing for himself, the gift of joyful contentment comes naturally, for in such a life of selfless giving there are few real disappointments. Limits and frustration cease to exist, for there is always some direction in which a loving heart can pour itself out.

It was a premeditated ladder—an ideal carefully thought out and held to through life. It was probably consciously formulated on a certain sea voyage when somewhere near the Equator he was lying in his hot cabin and he switched on the electric fan. He noticed that, in starting up, the fan made a good deal of noise but little breeze came from it. Later on at high power the fan was practically invisible and almost soundless, but the cabin was filled with a delicious airy breeze and the young man in his bunk prayed passionately that he might be like that electric fan, powerful for God yet self effacing; and with this in view he kept under his body and brought it into subjection.

And to this end he disciplined himself rigorously in matters of bodily appetite, the use of his time, his hours of sleep and his methods of recreation. For years he never had any breakfast, except a cup of tea, and he broke this habit at the end on medical advice only. He was a consistently early riser. He liked to listen to his wife reading good books aloud to the children, and he often played games with them, but he himself seldom read fiction and had no hobby beyond his work, which to him was in itself joy and relaxation; nor did he ever go in for any sort of sport, except swimming, although he was a great walker and would cheerfully start out in the early afternoon to walk seventeen miles to an evening meeting. As an old man he always gave one the impression of enjoying life so much that these restrictions were barely noticeable, but as a young man they must have loomed large.

He disciplined his time, too. Many people came to talk to him on spiritual matters, and they always found him intensely sympathetic and accessible. But once the point had been reached and the issue faced, he would gently but firmly close the interview. "Let's ask the Lord about it," he would say, and dropping on one knee he would pour out his heart to God and then courteously say goodbye. For gossip and pointless small talk he had no time whatsoever, and at certain types of tea-table he was not always quite a social success. He would quietly withdraw, mentally, into some green pasture of his own when he should have been making suitable replies about the weather.

And the systematic discipline of always seeking out the lowest place and the hardest way made him a very humble man. "Humble beyond the ordinary," wrote one who frequently traveled with him. "We have known him walk from the station carrying a case to join a group of men, any one of whom would have counted it an honor to have met him at the station. He would then slip into the room, scarcely noticeable in his entrance to the house." And to this man, so emptied of pomp and ceremony, so at leisure from himself, men were irresistibly drawn. Here was someone who had time for them and who would not despise them. An older man who attended the Grittleton Conference in 1949 has a memory of Mr. St. John that became a turning-point in his life. The Conference was mostly for young people and the older man may have felt a little out of it, until he met Mr. St. John pacing one of the long corridors of that beautiful country house. "Mr. St. John placed his arm across my shoulders," wrote this man years later, "and for about fifteen minutes we walked up and down. Somehow the conversation led him to discover that I was a railway man and expecting to retire, and I evidently said, which was true, that I had seen little apparent spiritual fruit in my life. Mr. St. John looked me in the face and said, 'My brother, you may have another fifteen years of service for the Lord, and you may find them the most fruitful of all, I think!' And the years of my life since then have been the most fruitful of all."

Men were drawn, too, not only because Mr. St. John was at leisure from himself, but because they knew that he loved them. It was the love that believed all things and hoped all things; hoped so deeply that he tended to see people through rose colored spectacles. He was sometimes exploited and taken in, but this did not upset him unduly and it was strangely rare. Far more often the evil was stemmed by the very impact of his trustful love, and men tended to become what he believed them to be.

A case in point was when through the unwise business dealings of one man a whole group got into difficulties about some church property. The landowner was an exceedingly grasping woman, and a lawsuit or severe financial loss threatened. There was much heated discussion and Mr. St. John, who had been in no way involved, offered to visit the woman, and having with great difficulty gained admission, he found himself in a little home bearing marks of deep poverty, and a sick child lying on the bed. Very little was said about the financial problem, much about the sick child, and by the end of the visit the woman was in tears, pouring out her sad story of bereavement and sickness and sin. Mr. St. John visited her again with a Bible, material help, and story books for the little girl. Without any further discussion the woman proposed a reasonably honest transaction. He grieved deeply over that woman in her poverty and sorrow, and thought and spoke much of her in the days that ensued, for to him every individual was intensely important. He was a man whose heart yearned over the multitudes, and once in an opening prayer at a Birkenhead Conference, he asked God's rich blessing on all those who spent their lives for the comfort of others: "The lamplighter who lights our streets for us, the miners who go down into the bowels of the earth to bring the coals to warm us on these winter nights, the fishermen who brave all weathers to bring us food, the navy who protect our coast so that we can gather fearlessly." His loving heartfelt gratitude embraced them all, and how yearningly would he reach out to seek to find some point of spiritual contact with his fellow-men. He was standing at the door of a Gospel Tent, inviting people in, when an elderly gentleman approached and declined Mr. St. John's invitation very courteously on the grounds that he was on the way to the exposition of the holy sacrament.

"Tell me," said Mr. St. John eagerly, "what does the blood of Christ mean to you?" "It means everything," replied the stranger, "for time and eternity." And he went his way, but Mr. St. John often spoke of the joy of that sudden moment of communion. "At the Cross our paths diverged," he would say, "but we met there if at no other point."

He was gloriously hospitable. "Do drop in to tea," he would urge strange families at the Sunday morning meeting. Sometimes, however, he forgot to mention it at home and an enthusiastic crowd would arrive at the front door just as the family were finishing tea. ("I'm afraid you were expecting six but we are only four!") His wife was a genius at carrying off these situations, but his children rather spoiled her efforts by relapsing into helpless giggles. The family learned to be ready for anything, and Sunday tea became a standing joke. Nor was it only tea. Mr. George Goodman arrived with a bag, apparently invited and considering himself expected for the week-end. Mr. St. John had gone to Ireland.

Yet apart from these slight lapses of memory, he was the soul of courtesy at home and always treated his wife and daughters like queens. He loved to help in the house, but apart from looking after babies, at which he excelled, his domestic efforts were not always successful. Some rather elegant ladies were once expected to tea, and Mrs. St. John, who was not very well, went to rest after dinner, making Mr. St. John promise to wake her in time to prepare. She was only woken at the last minute by her beaming husband. "Nothing to worry about, darling," he proclaimed triumphantly. "All is ready," and he ushered her excitedly into the drawing room to a table laden with piles and piles of great, thick, sparsely buttered door-steps! The ladies were actually arriving. There was apologetic feminine whispering and laughter in the passage, but our guests were sports; they munched gallantly away and the party was a great success.

That innate, lowly charity forbade him to speak ill of any or to judge, unless it was directly his business to do so. A group of young men, aware of this characteristic, sought to test him once by discussing in front of him a certain individual who had been giving a great deal of trouble. "Mr. St. John," said one of them, turning suddenly on the hitherto silent listener, "tell us honestly, what do you think of Mr. X?" There was a pause. The thoughtful brown eyes twinkled. "What do I think of Mr. X?" he repeated. "I think he has a perfectly charming wife."

On another occasion the conversation drifted during a meal to another group who were causing controversy. Some spoke critically, until Mr. St. John suddenly spoke out. "I have heard that some of these men have been much used in evangelistic work and have helped some of God's saints in days gone by. Shall we just bow our heads in prayer?" And after he had thanked God for the way He had used them and had asked Him to bless them in further service, the conversation was shifted to a better subject.

He practised this method and preached it in a sermon he once delivered on the Judgment Seat of Christ. "We are absolutely bound to judge everything that takes place in our own churches and in our own private lives. These things we are bound to judge, but the moment we judge anything outside that sphere, our judgment is challenged. Perhaps it's something to do with the service of another man or company of Christians with which we are not identified. Then we are absolutely prohibited from issuing our judgment and we should keep our opinions to ourselves. For instance, some time ago there came to our town an evangelist, a man whose methods are not those to which I have been accustomed. A good man came to see me one day and said, 'Mr. St. John, isn't this terrible?'—and he began to tell me some of the extravagant, peculiar things this man had done. I said, 'My dear brother, stop. Tell me one thing: Is the man preaching Christ?' 'Well,' he said, 'I can't deny it.' 'Well,' I said 'let's get down on our knees and pray that God will bless this man's ministry and use him for the conversion of souls.'"

Just as he could not speak uncharitably, so did he hate hearing gossip. Nor would he ever tolerate secret, behind the back methods. His own method of approach he once declared when speaking on 1 Corinthians chapter 1, verses 10-17: "It hath been declared unto me by them which are of the household of Chloe."

"We don't know the first thing about Chloe, but some people in her household had told Paul some very discreditable stories about the Corinthians, and Paul gives the name of his informant. I am not a person who has the slightest appreciation of listening to scandal, and I have a very simple method when a man tells me a shabby story. I say, 'By the way, I might like to mention this. Have you any objection to my using your name as authority for the story?' 'Oh,' he often says, 'I wouldn't have my name mentioned for the world.' 'Then,' I say, 'please don't inflict me with it any further.' There are certain cases when, in a godly way, you have to listen and hear something to someone's discredit, but be sure of this, that you always give the name of the person who told you. They have no right to tell if they don't want their names mentioned. And unless you are prepared to be identified as a member of the household of Chloe, don't tell me any more, Paul would have said."

But when all was said and done, the most striking and obvious thing about Mr. St. John was his joyfulness. At first sight it may have appeared a matter of temperament, and he certainly was blessed with a remarkably even, sunny disposition and an exceedingly healthy body.

But the roots of his unshakable content and radiant joy went down deep below a mere surface enjoyment of his surroundings. His heart was fixed on the things that could not be shaken—his blessings, as he called them. And that was why he could enjoy his mere mercies with such liberty and freedom from anxiety.

"We have all of us considered at times, no doubt," he said when speaking of spiritual blessings in Ephesians, "the distinction which we may fairly make between our blessings and our mercies. I have good health, a wife next to none on earth, and five children who, as the Scotsman says, are no' so bad, and a great many other good things. But they are all mercies, and not what the Bible speaks of as blessings. I have some blessings, too. I have peace with God, eternal life, justification by faith, the love of my brethren, a home in heaven, and I could go on all the evening telling you of my blessings. Now what is the underlying distinction between mercies and blessings? Just this—mercies may be swept away in a moment by a bolt from the blue. Health, family, friends, may be swept away in a flash. You have no certain tenure of your mercies. But nothing in the universe of God can touch a single blessing God ever gave you. If you have eternal life, you have it for as long as God lives, and every blessing stands on the farther side of the death of Christ, and they are all secure in the death of God's Son."

So his joy was secure, and how earnestly he warned his hearers not to cast the anchor of their soul's joy in any earthly love or circumstance.

"I pray you beyond all else," he cried, as he closed his last address on the book of Revelation, "never let any earthly love have power to lift you up to heaven or to cast you down into the dust. Keep the love of Christ on the pedestal of your soul. Always have the holy of holies in which the light is burning day and night; and if in the providence of God He smites your life or mine and shatters some vessel inestimably dear, at the very worst it shall only be with you as it was with Mary in the garden, with her eyes too blinded to be able even to see the Lord; but when He called His own sheep by name and said, 'Mary,' she answered, 'Rabboni,' that is to say, my great Master.'"

He could say, too, in all simplicity and honesty that he had been set free from those things which in so many cases mar a Christian's joy—pride, jealousy, and all the complicated spoiling manifestations of the self-life. He did not often deliberately give a testimony or speak of himself; but some times his joy in Christ's deliverance just bubbled over spontaneously.

"You can do men around you no better service in life," he burst out in the middle of a talk on Psalm 107, "better than giving them a good job or a thousand pounds; you can tell them how Jesus Christ has blessed you and made you intensely happy and delivered you from sin, death, pride, indulgence. You are able to stand before men and tell them that, by the grace of God, you are free of these things, you are master of the man who walks beneath your hat, and Christ has made you happy, and the world will know it. What will men think of you if they see you going about looking intensely happy? I've had men challenge me on that ground. A man said to me, 'You're a fool, but I wish I'd got what you've got.' Of course he did. What have I got? I've reached an assured haven, I've come inside the breakwater behind the storms and got in living touch with Christ, and life has nothing like the joy of telling people round you what Christ has done."

Worry and anxiety mar many people's joy, but he did not worry. An intensely loving, practical, capable and far-seeing wife, plus an optimistic nature, no doubt contributed to his peace of mind, but he had learnt, too, the meaning of an imagination that stops at God. "Thou wilt keep him in double peace—the word is repeated and means superlative peace—whose imagination stops at Thee," was his favorite translation of Isaiah 26:3. "This means," he commented, "that when there is trouble, anxiety, fear, the common way is to look at the fear and the possible consequences, to lie awake at night wondering what will happen, looking down the dark lane of possibility until you drop wearily asleep with a headache, as you deserve. In this verse Isaiah brings God into the area of himself and refuses to see anything else. You say that is blindness; on the contrary, it is faith. If in difficulty, the thing is to go into the Lord's presence and say, 'Here are the real facts. I am not going to conjure up ghostly facts of what might happen; I lay the real trouble before Thee, and there my imagination stops. I decline to go any further than Thee.'"

And how he loved to discourse on the lion, the adder and the dragon of Psalm 91 verse 13. The lion represented the sudden crashing tragedies that spring upon a man; the adder the hidden bitternesses that attack and poison his spirit. "But," he would cry, his voice vibrant with triumph, "nobody ever saw a dragon in their lives. They are the things that might happen, but never do; and more lives are shadowed by the dragon than by any other beast."

But when testing and darkness did come, what then? For while his circumstances were outwardly happy, there were many conflicts and heartaches to do with the care of the churches, and in one of his sudden, vivid flashes of imagination, he once described his own reaction to grey days. He was actually speaking on the verse, "How shall we sing the song of the Lord in a strange land?" (Psalm 137:4).

"The Lord's song never sounds so sweetly as when sung in a strange land. All the noblest songs are born, not out of fine days, but out of tragic days, and the finest literature that the world possesses is in songs like these. Go back to the days of David in exile, John Bunyan in Bedford jail, Milton in his blindness, Samuel Rutherford in his banishment, and you'll find that the singing of the Lord's songs is better in a strange land than anywhere else. The Lord Jesus did it. He sat by the side of the sea, and as He watched the foam of death He sang; He sang as He left the upper room, and when He came out of death He sang the Lord's song in the land of resurrection. A strange land! He'd never been there before. Stephen sang the Lord's song when they were stoning him. He said, 'I see Jesus up there.' Saul of Tarsus, over sixty years of age, has been seized and thrust into the stocks, and at midnight he says, 'Silas, how about a bit of the Lord's song?' Silas might say, 'This is not the time and place; let us wait till we get to the meeting.' But no, they sang it then and there, and the result was that the jailor was converted and all the prisoners heard it."

It was an ever-apparent song, rising from depths of praise that spilled over in a sparkling enjoyment of life's pleasures. And this increased as he grew older. A friend always remembers their last meeting in London—old Mr. St. John sitting on the grass in St. James's Park, enjoying the sunshine and the picnic like a schoolboy. Often during the war he would come and take his daughter out from hospital, and, not really at home in any red-tape atmosphere and probably dreaming of the prophets, he once unconsciously seated himself on a seat in Outpatients forbidden by large notices to the public. Sister hurried up, all starch and indignation, but his beaming innocence disarmed even that lady and she retired smiling. He was so certain she had come to welcome him to her domain, so cordially delighted to be there. Then he and his daughter would sally forth to Kew Gardens, or a trip up the Thames, and his radiant pleasure in the expedition would banish for a few hours all the horror and strain of the war and the wounded and the raided nights. She would go back feeling strangely refreshed and balanced.

The song was the outward expression of his quiet, deep content in whatever circumstances he happened to find himself, and it had nothing whatever to do with things or comforts. "Always remember," he once said, "we are the followers of a Christ Who on earth had a peasant's lot, slept upon a hillside, and if He wanted to illustrate His preaching had to borrow a penny with which to do it. And yet His heart was full of the Father's joy and gladness; and if you walk with God that joy will stay your hearts and set them free from things around you."

There never was a moment right up to the last when he could not look trustfully up to God and say, "The lines are fallen to me in a pleasant place, yea, I have a goodly heritage." In a lecture on the sixteenth Psalm he once enlarged on that very verse. "In the land tenure of Palestine it was usual to re-distribute the land every few years. Here are the fields: one side is rocky and the other side fertile. It's not fair that one family should always have the fertile or the sterile portion, so there was a fresh allotment every few years. Now, says David, 'The lot is cast into the lap' . . . 'The lines have fallen unto me in pleasant places' . . . 'But Thou hast not where to lay Thy head.' 'Pleasant places,' says Christ. 'But Lord, You dwelt for thirty years in a crowded little cottage and You were despised and spat upon!' 'The lines are fallen unto Me in pleasant places,' says Messiah, and who but He would ever say it? And the next time there are things we should like different, what should we say?—'Lord, whose hand was it that cast the lot? Who won me that sterile piece to bring fertility out of it? Who gave me that easy bit for a certain part of my life? Thou maintainest my lot . . . I have a goodly heritage.' Think of the Lord Jesus looking up into His Father's face and saying, 'You have given me a wonderful heritage.' What was it? A dozen fishermen, the world's scorn and contempt, and the Cross.

But He looked ahead and saw the joy that was set before Him and said, 'Father, it is a goodly heritage.'"

This joy attracted, and his goodwill made the attraction mutual. It was inevitable that, with seeing such thousands of people, he should often forget those with whom he had only had a passing though true spiritual communion. Yet in each country he visited he gathered to his heart a few names that he would never forget—names of men, young and old, who enriched his whole life with their friendship. There was Mr. Wanhill who knew him as a young man in the Bank, and who wrote, after sixty-two years of unbroken friendship, "Surely a love over so many years will be renewed and continued in our Father's house; it cannot die."

There was Mr. Robert Laidlaw in New Zealand, whose goodness to Mr. St. John's whole family down the years has been unsurpassed; Mr. Rice H. Clayton in Australia, to whom Mr. St. John sent almost his last love and messages; Richard Hill, the Trotters and the Loizeauxs in the States, the Sheppards and Mr. Bowen in Canada; Dr. Northcote Deck, who reached heaven the day before he did; beloved Mr. Payne and Mr. Lear in the Argentine; Mr. McNair and Mr. Ellis in Brazil; the Flanigans and the Matthews in Ireland (and how he treasured the big family photograph of the Matthews children, always on his bookshelf); Mr. Robert Balloch in Scotland, with whom he corresponded fully and freely throughout the years, exchanging the spoil of their studies and the love of their hearts.

There was something rare and beautiful about these friendships, some of which were old-age ones that had stood the test of many years. As young men some of them had strengthened each other's hands in God, and as old men the links of devotion, gratitude, mutual respect and inspiration had become even more firmly welded, and they did not attempt to conceal it. Long since purged of all rivalry or emulation, these old fellow-laborers in the gospel could pour out their love for each other without complex or reserve. What a light is thrown on the friendship and fellowship of many years by the following letter, written by Mr. W. E. Vine in his old age to Mr. St. John:

"I must proceed at once to correct the wrong impression conveyed in your letter, the love of which I deeply appreciate. You speak of a large debt of love and fellowship and help lying to my credit in your ledgers. By what mental process you have arrived at a transmutation of such details from the debit to the credit side I do not know. I am confident that the figure in my own ledgers is right, and that in my books your credit side is full and the debit practically empty. What I owed you during the years I have known you cannot be set out in a letter. Your ministry of precept and practice, instruction and example, would fill many pages. I do not remember having had such a variety of difficult questions to answer as we have had in the week that is past, and yet what harmony over the whole period. Here again the figures in my ledger loom large; grace, patience, forbearance and a readiness to reserve an expression of opinion, even when you might perhaps reasonably have contradicted me."

As Mr. St. John grew older, he loved to pour out his friendship on the younger men who ministered with him, and who, as his strength failed, were beginning to take his place. Of the close, lasting friendships in his own country there is neither space nor time to tell. Dozens of cherished names leap to one's mind. Most of the larger towns, and many small ones, held dear human associations for him. There was one friendship cut short by sudden death (which Mr. St. John never quite got over)—that of Mr. Fred Mitchell, the Home Director of the China Inland Mission. They had not known each other for more than a dozen years, nor seen each other very often, but they had loved deeply and closely and shared each other's burdens. It was only a short while before his death that Mr. Mitchell wrote of his plans, and ended his letter by saying: "I do hope you will be back at Abergele for the prayer conference, if for no other reason than that I may have some time with you. You are to me a brother beloved; I am always helped heavenwards when I have a little time with you. I hope it is not selfish. I continue to pray much for every member of your family, and thank God that ever I came to know you. With continuing and deepening love."

The news of the fatal plane crash in May, 1953, was a tremendous blow to Mr. St. John. "I have lost my dearest friend of his generation," he wrote to one of his children. "I saw him seldom, but I have rare memories of times of deep, urgent prayer. It was one of the strongest friendships of my life, and for several days I felt stunned. I had to write and tell you, but how rich I am with so many on the other side."

And later on, "I sent you the account of Fred's Memorial Service; it still seems quite unreal to me. He has been such a close part of my heart and life that it will take a long time to grasp that he has really gone Home. When our Lord was here, He recognized no break in life: 'He that believeth in me shall never die.' Death, to Him, was just an incident in continuity. In His mind people did not go to an idle heaven, but passed on into a life of unbroken service. 'Faithful over few things . . . enter thou into the joy . . . I will make thee ruler.'"

He knew much of the responsibilities and rewards of friendship, and he held the responsibilities sacred. "Abraham, the friend of God," he once said, "and if God esteems His friends, has He given us any? If so, how have we treated them? Have we held them, or carelessly allowed them to be lost? If so, what answer will you give on the day of accountability? If He gives you what He Himself esteems, treasure it."

And of its reward, he knew all about that, too. As a young man he had written in the old diary, "Oh the comfort, the inexpressible relief of feeling safe with a person, having neither to measure thought or weigh words, but to pour out all, chaff and grain together, knowing that a faithful friend sifts out what is worth keeping, and with the breath of kindness blows the rest away."

And how much of Harold St. John's life was spent sifting. How swiftly he forgot the chaff and with what glowing joy he treasured the wheat.

CHAPTER 13

The Preacher

A BIOGRAPHER who attempts to follow up Harold St. John's movements from about 1925 to 1955 is confronted with no easy task. He kept no diary nor any record of dates, and those that have been supplied are only approximate and spasmodic. He appears to leap from continent to continent with ease and rapidity and to have visited hundreds of places. Yet there are certain centers and conferences where he ministered regularly and round which other activities partly revolved. For many consecutive summers during the nineteen-twenties and early thirties he lectured in the United States and in Canada. He loved to think back to the early days at Seacliff Conferences with Richard Hill. He visited Rhodes Grove, the Stony Brook School, Greenwood Hills, Pennsylvania, and other summer gatherings. He held meetings in Los Angeles and in various centers in the USA. Up in Canada he gave a series of powerful addresses on the present spiritual value of the Book of the Revelation, and also for many years he wrote the editorials and other articles in Mrs. Fitch's magazine, *The Bible Scholar.*

He loved the States, and even considered taking his family and making his home there, as he was at one time offered the head-ship of a well-known Bible College. He turned down the offer after much thought and prayer, but the land and its people attracted him irresistibly. He felt utterly at home in the warm, genial, unconventional atmosphere, and of the unfailing kindness of those American friends much could be written, specially during the war years. With their characteristic large-heartedness they adopted him and his family as their own, and now four years after his death there is still many a close, unbroken link of prayer and fellowship between Mr. St. John's wife and children and his friends in the States.

He twice visited New Zealand, in 1934 and 1937, though he went once only to Australia, in 1937. Later in his life he had hoped to go again, though this wish was never realized. He enjoyed the boundless hospitality of Messrs. Robert Laidlaw, H. C. Hewlett, John Burrows and J. S. Burt in New Zealand, and was vitally associated with the Camp Movement that has so rapidly developed since and become such a source of blessing to the Christian youth of New Zealand. He was the chief speaker at Brown's Bay Summer Camp, and one who remembers him there writes:

"I was just in the second year of my married life when I first met your father. I have photographs taken of him at one of the early Bible Class Camps we had at Brown's Bay, which has been the forerunner of our extensive Camp Movement throughout New Zealand. I think that would be the Christmas of the year 1934. There is a photo in which he is a prisoner at a mock trial. I remember that I had to defend him on that occasion for the great offence of having stolen our hearts. I have still another photo of him in his pyjamas. It was his habit to rise in the Camp about six, stroll along the pier in the early morning sunshine thus attired, reading his Testament. I had the opportunity of spending quite a good deal of time in your father's company, and these impressions remain.

"The long walks he would take with a few of us when we discoursed intimately together and he gave us out of the rich fount of his own spiritual experience, are unforgettable; the luncheons we arranged in a city tea-room when a group of about eight or ten of us would lunch with him, and the conversation would roam over many spiritual topics. We were all in the late twenties or early thirties at the time, and those who lunched with him then are all now prominent in the assembly life and activities of the city.

"Apart from these personal reminiscences, I would say that the general impressions left by your father's two visits to New Zealand were these—the quality and depth of his knowledge of Holy Scripture, the courtesy and chivalry of his gracious manner, and the disciplined life that he led. What impressed me, personally, was the absence in his speech of any criticism of his fellow-Christians, the sunny, radiant personality of one who enjoyed his Christian life with a zest, and who inspired others to follow his example and walk in the things of God. I have not the least overdrawn this picture; it was what we all felt about him."

He arrived in Australia in time to share the platform with Mr. Alfred Gibbs for the Easter meetings in Melbourne. He also visited Sydney, Adelaide and Tasmania. He stayed a month in Melbourne, and the pattern of those days is well remembered by his host, Mr. R. H. Clayton: "Up soon after six, cold bath, one cup of tea for breakfast, a glance at the paper. Work till lunch, then visiting. Dinner here or else where, ministry in the evenings." (It was the generous love of the brethren in Australia, New Zealand and the States in sending food parcels during the war years that was the largest factor in making it possible for his wife to keep open house for members of the Forces.)

In the British Isles he had certain regular haunts. Between the years 1922 and 1954 he gave thirty addresses at the Bloomsbury Central Church meetings, the greater number being given during the last twelve years of his life. For eight years he conducted afternoon Bible Readings, for which about two hundred people would gather in the lower part of the Church. He would draw his chair to the front of the platform and talk, sitting—a concession to advancing years. Part of a chapter would be expounded and questions invited; if relevant and important, fully answered; if trivial or irrelevant, gently but firmly set aside.

One of his last meetings at Bloomsbury was memorable. It was plain that he was deeply moved towards the close of his address and broke out into burning words of personal testimony, strangely reminiscent of Polycarp's confession:

"For sixty years He has been my greatest, dearest Friend; He's never let me down," and more in the same strain. Later it transpired that his keen eye had seen in the audience a group of young people brought up in Christian homes but as yet, he believed, without Christ. It was an appeal to them, perhaps his last.

At South Park Chapel, Seven Kings, he ministered annually, if in England, over a period of about forty-five years. He was originally drawn there by the founder, Mr. W. H. Knox, for whose practical Christianity he had a profound admiration. Mr. St. John often gave 25-30 addresses a year to that particular meeting. He ministered the Word over a wide area in Scotland during many years, also visiting the large New Year conferences in various centers. He had a special interest in the weeks of Bible Readings that were held at Netherhall, Largs, at

Ayr and at Aberdeen, and at different times he shared the responsibility for those gatherings with Messrs. C. F. Hogg, J. B. Watson, J. M. Shaw, W. W. Fereday, G. C. D. Howley and George Harpur. Long after he was unable to travel, his heart yearned for the Largs conference, and at the beginning of May, 1957, he sent a telegram to those who had gathered at the Annual Bible Reading. "Isaiah 38:19 and 20. Harold St. John." These were the words sent by a dying man, and they were read aloud: "The living, the living, he shall praise thee, as I do this day: the father to the children shall make known thy truth. The Lord was ready to save me: therefore we will sing my songs to the stringed instruments all the days of our life in the house of the Lord." The telegram crossed their greeting to him—a gay picture postcard of Scottish Highlanders in full uniform, marching forward to the sound of drums and bagpipes. It arrived at mid-day on May 11th—just as the gates were opening and Harold St. John was marching joyfully forward into the presence of his King.

It was at Seven Kings first of all, and later at Largs, that he gave, on request, an account of his own conversion and early spiritual life, a subject he very rarely spoke of. "No one felt like going to bed," said one who had attended the meeting at Largs. "Lights were supposed to be out at 11 p.m., but little groups sat in the dark in bedrooms and talked until the early hours of the morning. Six of us sat in our bedroom until after 1 a.m., wondering of what use our lives were, after what we had just heard."

His love for Northern Ireland was a later development. But at the Bible Study Group in Portballintrae in 1949 the place was packed out, and again in Portrush. He ministered for many years at the Summer Schools at Plas Menai, Llanfairfechan, in North Wales, at the Reading Conference and at the Conventions in Bournemouth. He preached on the Keswick platform in London. Up and down the length and breadth of the country he traveled, and wherever he preached there was a lifting-up of men's hearts and a new hunger and thirst after holiness. Many have tried to describe the peculiar quality of his preaching or the effect it had on them. One young man who lived at Wrexham, in North Wales, used to cycle night after night to Liverpool and back, after a hard day's work in the coal mines, when Mr. St. John was giving a series of lectures. Another in Scotland went reluctantly to his first lecture on being told that the subject was the book of Habakkuk, but he heard an address that so opened his eyes that he spent his next year of Bible study absorbed in the minor prophets.

"Everything he touched took on some fresh hue and the rich vein of poetry in his nature produced the most vivid imagery in his preaching," wrote one who often shared a platform with him. "His intonation of voice and interpretation of Scripture were peculiarly his own, although it was not merely the spoken word that made such an impression on his listeners; many preachers knew their Bibles, but Mr. St. John knew his Lord."

"His ministry was unique," wrote one of the leaders of his own home meeting at Malvern. "His grasp of Scripture was telescopic and microscopic. He took the telescope of his God-inspired knowledge and swept the infinite realm of Scriptures and vast expanses and discovered to the saints many a star of truth. He moved amidst the immensities and we sought to hitch our chariots to the stars, and our souls were lit up and our minds illuminated. But when he picked up the microscope and called upon us to look through it, we saw fresh glory in the smallest flowers of the Word, dainty touches, tender tones in exquisite language, which all combined to make this detailed exegesis of Scripture most effective."

What was the secret of such power and such influence in preaching? The answer is probably a complex one. The hours of concentrated study he put into his preparation has already been enlarged upon, and not only study, but long patient thought, so that his subject matter was sometimes the mature, ripened outcome of years of cogitation and experience.

"Many years ago," he said at the opening of a series of lectures on Job, "I began my first careful reading of the book of Job and worked my way through thirty-seven chapters to the end of Elihu's ministry, giving, as far as I could, attention to every word, verse and speech. Then with high hopes I turned to read the speeches of Jehovah, and for the first and last time of my dealings with Scripture I suffered profound disappointment. There was nothing there that I had expected. I was looking for profound philosophic interpretations of the ministries of suffering in this world. I found nothing in the speeches of the blessed God except details of the creation and the habits of seven beasts about which I knew nothing. I closed the Book and said, 'This is not for me,' and I was right. It only worked out its philosophy years later, and I find now that as long as life lasts I have, in those chapters, every bit of light and mental healing I shall ever need when I stand perplexed before the ministries of suffering."

Then his technique, his wealth of matter, and his originality of expression were unusual, and even his announcement of his subject was worded in an arresting fashion.

Galatians 5—"The Factory and the Garden."

Addresses on the four Gospels—"The Tax Collector and the King," "The Levite and his Lord," "The Physician and his Priest," "The Fisherman and his God."

Lectures on the book of Numbers—"The Camp of the Saints."

Lectures on the four major prophets—"The Thrones and the Live Coal," "The Almond Rod and the Cauldron," "The Living Cherubim and the Wheels," "By Pulse and Prayer."

His opening sentence too was often designed to surprise the listeners into attention. "We'll turn to the book of Ezekiel—a pasture where the sheep of God are not often found grazing." Or, "I am the owner of many umbrellas in many parts of the world; I am the possessor of none of them." This last provided a vivid introduction to the subject of possessing your possessions, in the Epistle to the Ephesians.

His way of speaking was completely natural and entirely free from pedantry. He was occasionally more imaginative than correct, as when, carried away by his subject, he pictured Paul drawing out his watch and telling Silas that it was midnight and time for a song, but this never worried him. When told one day that the famous Dr. Jowett had had a sleepless night remembering how he had mixed his metaphors, Mr. St. John replied kindly, "He need not have worried; the Lord mixed His metaphors. Didn't He say, 'Fear not, little flock, it is your Father's good pleasure to give you the kingdom'?"

Many parts of the Bible have been permanently lit up to his audience by the vividness of his imaginative telling. Surely no-one could ever forget the New Testament teaching on immature Christians after the following outbursts:

"In 1 Corinthians chapter 3, verses 1 to 3, the church is a nursery, and Paul is feeding the babies. Verses 4 to 9a, the church suddenly changes into a garden; Paul has a spade and is planting, while Apollos runs round with the watering-can. Paul says, I came to Corinth as a mother-nurse, and I gave you the best milk I could get, and it was all very well when you were infants and milk was the proper diet; but every day I looked at the chart and thought you should give up this milk, for I have any amount of strong meat nicely cooked and prepared; but your eye went to the bottle and you hadn't a single idea beyond that bottle. I had the finest of the wheat and the best things God has got for you, but there you were with your stagnated minds always twisting round that bottle. The cause of that is found in verse 3; you were still like that, having known Christ for several years. And the reason is, you are jealous of one another and don't get on together, and walk as if you were men, whereas you should walk as saints, growing in grace and the knowledge of the Lord Jesus Christ. And isn't that really one of the tragedies of the modern Church? How many of us as Christians are content to go on feeding on the same Scriptures, praying the same prayers, thinking about the same things, and God would have us go from strength to strength, from twilight to the noonday sun. The little child who declines to grow up is the first illustration, like Peter Pan.

"Now you must not forget there are other babies in the New Testament—two others. Turn to Peter in passing: 1 Peter 1 verse 23, the baby is born. 'Being born again, not of corruptible seed, but of incorruptible, by the Word of God, which liveth and abideth for ever.' Then in chapter 2:2, 'As newborn babes, desire the sincere milk of the word that ye may grow thereby.' And if you do grow, what will happen? You will want stronger food, when you learn that the Lord is gracious. That is a delightful baby; it has not got any idea but one, and that is, it needs milk and knows where to go and get it.

"Now turn to Hebrews 5, where you find another baby spoken of: 'For when by reason of the time ye ought to be teachers, ye have need again that some one teach you the rudiments of the first principles of the oracles of God; and are become such as have need of milk, and not of solid food. For every one that partaketh of milk is without experience of the word of righteousness; for he is a babe. But solid food is for full grown men, even those who by reason of use have their senses exercised to discern good and evil.' (Verses 12 to 14, R.V.) Is that like the Corinthian baby? Not in the least. Here they are, all sitting in their high chairs. The first one is sitting there with his bottle and he is healthy; a few months old and as happy as can be. Peter's baby desires the sincere milk of the word. The Corinthian baby is still at his bottle, but to him it is a disgrace. The worst of all is one sitting there, who is about forty-five years old. There was a day when he used to eat strong meat, but he's gone back and become one who needs milk. The first is normal, the second's stunted—he's never grown up, but the third is positively diseased and has gone back; he used to eat strong meat, but in the passage of years he has gone back to spiritual childhood, a terrible specimen of senile decay. All these classes of people are found in churches; and do be careful that you have a daily dissatisfaction with the things with which you first started. Don't throw them over, but learn to feed on stronger, deeper things as life goes on. So says the Apostle, here in our passage. The nursery is all out of order and the children decline to develop."

And no listener could ever again be in doubt as to the contents of Romans 11 after hearing Mr. St. John's triumphant summary:

"The Jewish train has been shunted into a siding, and the Church express comes thundering through; and the Jew says, 'I wish I were on that.' My dear fellow, you may be; there's plenty of room on the train. 'There are those people being wafted to heaven on that express,' he says; 'I should like to join them.' And the time will come, says Paul, when he will join them. God will work on their hearts and they will turn back to God."

Or the following: "Do you wonder that Daniel hesitated or thought twice about a den of mangy lions in a subterranean cavern? In point of view of time, chapter eight came before chapter six, and Daniel had seen a beast that *was* a beast, not a commonplace creeper of Babylon."

Or could anyone fail to take this vivid rebuke to heart?—"The Church could evangelize the world, if awake. But she lies in her dormitories, drugged with sectarianism."

His preaching was rich in illustration which he drew from history, literature, travel, science and from his own personal experience in all parts of the world. It lit up all his teaching and made it wonderfully attractive. "Your doctrine must be lifted up into the sunlight," he once said. And with moving effect he could weave the teaching of the ancient poets into modern evangelical truth.

"Dante takes his pilgrims through the unseen world, and when the journey is nearly finished, he brings his pilgrim to a place where there are two rivers and says to him, 'You must drink of both. If you drink of one, you will forget all the sins and sorrows of your past; if you drink of the other, there shall be graven upon the tablets of your memory, as long as life lasts, all the goodness and mercy and discipline of God.' Now that shows great insight in Dante, for there are two things we need. 'I will remember thy sin no more,' and 'Thou shalt remember all the way that the Lord thy God led thee.' And if a man gets a good drink from these two rivers he will never sink into the depths; but you can only find those streams and rivers by the mingling of a sinner's tears and a Saviour's blood."

He had a tremendous sense of the high calling and dignity of the ministry and often advised young men to take heed and count the cost before they embarked on preaching, although he loved to share the platform with them and would listen with deep consideration to all they had to say.

"Preachers are always kings," he once told them, "but lest I should have you leaping to your feet to deliver yourselves speedily of some new thought on Romans, may I say this to my young friends who have honored me with their confidence: do not be in too much of a hurry to take up this tremendous task of preaching. Remember that preaching demands long months and years of spiritual toil, and a preacher who starts too young (though I cannot help but think of Charles Spurgeon, whom nobody could keep down at the age of sixteen) very largely makes his reputation in the first two or three years of his public ministry; and if, as is the case very often in early life, you are crude in speech and bare in knowledge, without much experience, people will accord you a certain reputation in your early youth that will very often follow you. I'm not speaking of the sufferings of your audience; I'm only reminding you of this: that you make your reputation in your earliest days when you begin to preach, and all through your life there will cling to you certain things; so do not be in a hurry. Your Lord Jesus began to preach when He was thirty years old, Paul when he was nearly forty, John the Baptist about twenty-nine, so don't be in a hurry to make a reputation over which you and your friends may blush in later years."

"And," he said another time, in a more solemn vein, "let us see that we don't *imagine* that we are all called to stand up and preach, and don't suppose that the mere fact that we wear coats and trousers gives us the moral right to inflict our words on our fellow-saints. Do remember that the ministry of the Word is an intensely solemn thing, and God keep you in this time from what is known as the brother with the little word. My dear brethren, the ministry of the Word is God speaking through anointed men by the Holy Spirit, and we have no right to insult the intelligence and fritter away the time of a hundred people, unless the Lord has given us some definite opening of Holy Scripture in the power of the Holy Ghost."

Not only did he urge restraint on the young men, but also on the old men whose powers of expression were declining. He himself resigned from the eldership of the local assembly at a much earlier age than most thought necessary. "The art of growing old gracefully is one which the writer finds great pleasure in practising," he wrote in an article on the service of the Levites. "If the time has come to surrender any heavy form of service, it is useless to accept one's own judgment, still less that of one's wife. The most spiritual man available will give us better counsel. In Christian work we who are older must remember that the bulk of the public platform work will be done by our younger brethren. A man may be an admirable preacher at fifty, a passable one at sixty, a bore at seventy and a positive nuisance at eighty. There are, of course, many exceptions, of which the late Dr. A. T. Pierson was a conspicuous case."

"Spirit-filled ministry"—that was his secret, and he never depended in the least on his technique or his originality of diction or even on his carefully prepared material. He loved to tell the story of an American who came to England to hear a great preacher, and heard him speak morning, afternoon, and evening; but his heart was not touched. Going back to his hotel he was attracted by a crowd, and an uneducated young man was speaking in the open air, and there was something about that young man that gripped the American, especially one sentence of his preaching. "Friends," said the young man, "I've never been to College but I've been to Calvary." And hearing this story of Calvary the visitor got the thrill for which he had come to London.

"And may I say," added Mr. St. John, "that the Cross of our Lord Jesus Christ never means a thing to us until it takes our breath away and becomes the biggest thing in life. It's not what we see, but what we feel in life. I must feel the power of the gospel and see the Cross in a personal way, or I had better not talk about it."

He enlarged on this utter dependence on the Spirit of God in a lecture he gave on 1 Corinthians chapter 2: "There are three things you have got to learn, Paul says, in this passage, verses 10 to 16; and let me say that there is not a passage a preacher needs to study with greater insistence and greater care than 1 Corinthians 2, verses 10 to 16. Because you see, in preaching there are three things. First, the preacher must know the truth; and how is he to get it? By revelation from the Spirit of God. Secondly, he must have words in which to clothe his sermon. Where is he to get them? You say he has a good style and is a fluent speaker. Paul says that won't do. The words in which he clothes his thoughts must come from the same Spirit. Thirdly, how about the people who are listening? Paul says you have to have the Spirit in them also to whom you speak. The natural man is not capable of understanding spiritual things; so the ideas must come from God, the words and the preparation of heart for the message must come from God. Why, you say, this preaching business doesn't make anything of me! That is exactly what it is meant to do—to make nothing of you. The ideas reach you by the Spirit's ministry; He searches those things; the words come from Him, and the man listening has the ability to understand only as the Spirit gives it. That is a tremendous passage for a preacher. I don't know any that searches me as this one does.

"How does he work his material out? Verses 10 to 12: the natural man is absolutely incapable of getting hold of, receiving or understanding the deep things of God. Well then, how can I know? Verse 10: God reveals them by His Spirit. 'For the Spirit searcheth all things, yea the deep things of God.' Very well then, the Spirit knows them, but how am I to get them? Verse 12: 'We received not the spirit of the world but the Spirit which is of God, that we might know the things that are freely given to us by God.' It may be worth noticing in passing that the two words 'knoweth,' in verse 11, represent very different ideas. They are quite different words as Paul wrote them. The first is the ordinary word for general knowledge, speaking of an ordinary man; but at the end of the verse it is quite another word, not the present tense but the perfect tense, meaning nobody can come to know or enter into, by thought, prayer, or desire, these things, excepting by the Holy Ghost Who will reveal those things freely given to us of God. So the first paragraph says there is no way of finding out definite truth except by the revelation of the Holy Ghost, the Holy Spirit in the believer.

"And so now you have your sermon in your mind, and you are walking to the preaching place. You say, I have wonderful ideas, but have you any words in which to clothe your wonderful ideas? You'd better go to the same source for the words as you did for the thoughts—verse 13—'Which things also we speak, not in the words which man's wisdom teacheth, but which the Holy Ghost teacheth.' But, you say, I thought I had to go to the schools, and be careful not to pronounce a word wrongly or have a faulty construction in grammar, using the English language with great deftness and dexterity. I dare say Peter on the day of Pentecost may have made a dozen grammatical mistakes, his accent may have been deplorable, but he preached in ways and thoughts that the Holy Ghost supplied, and three thousand people were saved under his preaching. D. L. Moody smashed and trampled on every rule of English grammar, and broke the King's English into fragments, but scores would come to the Lord Jesus because Moody went to God for his messages and for the words in which to clothe his message. Well, as you said, it is all right, everything is ship-shape. You have the message and the thoughts. Now, says Paul, don't be in any hurry—verse 14—You have to find out something else. Are you going to preach to a brick wall? Let us understand this word, the natural man. It was coined by Aristotle, and he uses it in a very striking way. He said there are two kinds of men: those swayed by physical desires, the drunkard and the man of immoral life; and then the highest type of man—a man swayed by his soul. He may have a thirst for knowledge and that's a noble thing, and so says Aristotle, that is the natural man. The natural man is the man who can discover the treasures of scientific knowledge; but Paul says you may have a whole room full to listen to you and they won't make head or tail of your message until something happens. Neither the highest type of intellectual, or the degraded and the debased, can receive the things of the Spirit of God, for they are foolishness unto him, neither can he know them because they are spiritually discerned—that is to say, until the Spirit of God gets to work in him. You say, I am going to preach a fine sermon, but you won't get anywhere unless the Spirit begins to work upon your listener's soul and he is born of the Spirit. All your fine words will be lost unless that happens. Of course you have to preach the gospel, but you must always remember that if you are facing five hundred people unconverted, there may be ten with whom the Spirit has begun to work. He awakens them and then convicts them of sin, and then your words come in like healing balm. But the Spirit must be there."

And because of this utter dependence on the Spirit day by day, the guidance and the teaching of the Spirit were so evident in his life. He seldom preached the same sermon twice. "The gold he brought forth from the divine treasury was always fresh minted," said one of his listeners; and he himself likened the Spirit of God to an ever-flowing river. "The river of God never runs dry," he said. "You never need have stale, out-of-date ministry or preaching that bores the Lord's people. You need never be like the Gibeonites who brought to Joshua moldy bread and split wineskins. Joshua should have known at once that the Lord never sent them. Joshua should have said, 'The Lord never gave you wineskins like that.' No, if the Spirit of God is flowing, you will find the ministry always fresh, and the Lord gives that which is for the refreshing of His people.

"Again, every scribe that is instructed in the kingdom of God is like a householder, bringing forth from his treasures things new and old. What does that mean? That there should be a constant bringing out from the treasures of the soul, a living ministry adapted to the needs of God's people. Things new—we don't want men like gramophone records, always the same thing. We want a freshness in the ministry, a power that brings out new things, yes, things new and old. That is, new lines on all truths that strike their roots deep into the old eternal things. It must be new and old. So when you conclude an address, and some old brother shakes his head with pleasure and says, 'That's just what I was told forty years ago,' you say, 'Well, I'm glad you enjoyed it, but there was a word you did not hear forty years ago, because the Spirit of God reserved it for this servant today.' Every servant of God when he speaks, will have two things in his mind: first, a fresh picture of Christ, received from reading the passage; and then the background on which it rests, the landmarks which have stood since Pentecost. This is what makes the ministry attractive—that a man always has a fresh word from God. The center of the picture is the divine message given by the Spirit, and in the surrounding framework is the old truths we have known and loved."

Instantly sensitive to the guidance of the Holy Spirit, he occasionally altered his prepared message at the very last moment and spoke quite spontaneously. A fellow-minister, who shared the pulpit with him, remembers one of these incidents. "One year we were dealing with Elijah in the evening sessions at Ayr. I gave the opening address on this prophet, and Mr. St. John followed with a shorter message on Elisha. One evening I spoke on my theme, and was speaking on Elijah at Mount Carmel, and referred in passing to 1 Kings 18:44. When the time came for Mr. St. John to follow, he said he had felt strongly constrained to alter his message, and he was going to speak on the three occasions in which a man's hand was mentioned in the Old Testament. He read from 1 Kings 18, Ezekiel 1 and Daniel 5, and when he came to speak on the Daniel passage he gave a most powerful gospel appeal. After the meeting a man was converted, and it was felt that that was an instance of clear divine leading to alter an address, to meet a specific need in the congregation."

And because of the need for this continual filling of the Spirit, he kept himself as a man apart, a vessel fit for the Master's use. His whole life was a constant preparation. "I cannot recall a single occasion when he arrived late for a service," wrote one. He sought rest and preparation during the day, and his ministry was clearly fresh from the divine presence. His habit was to walk alone to the meeting, arriving a long time before the service began. If there was collective prayer, he was there. If not, he would find a quiet corner for prayer and contemplation, and when he ascended the platform there was a light on his face as of a man who had seen God, and in his opening prayer he seemed to draw the company with him into the presence of the Father. "Let us praise," he would say, and one of the opening utterances is remembered after a lapse of thirty years: "We came here tonight as students of Thy Word; may we leave as humble worshipers at the feet of our adorable and overflowing Saviour."

Prayer was the atmosphere in which his soul lived, and he practically never concluded any serious conversation without breaking forth into prayer. He spoke with God as naturally as to a well-loved friend, and the originality of his graces before meals was a constant surprise to family and guests. "For this food and for Mummy we praise and bless Thy Name," he once burst forth spontaneously. And he was absolutely uncompromising on the daily necessity for solitude and prayer.

"The Lord Jesus had a little ship whose exclusive service was to wait on Him. What was it for? 'Because of the multitude, lest they should throng Him.' The Lord is not going to have a life hemmed in by perpetual crowds, and that is the first thing a minister must see to—that he has a little ship close at hand, that his spirit always has a place of retreat. Christ also had a mountain where He often went. The little ship is always at hand; the mountain is for larger, withdrawn fellowship with God."

Not only did he prepare himself, but he sought to impress upon his audience the need of preparation and of humble, expectant approach. On one occasion a chairman had spoken in glowing, flattering terms of the good reputation and high spiritual level of the congregation Mr. St. John was about to address. When at last the chairman sat down, Mr. St. John rose to his feet. "I am honored to address such an audience," he said quietly. "May the Lord keep us all humble; you on your pedestals and me in my little ditch. Let us turn to the Scriptures."

He felt so deeply and strongly about this subject of preparation for the ministry that he wrote a small booklet entitled *Preparation for Service,* part of which is here quoted:

Since we are composed of three parts, body, soul and spirit, it may condense our thinking if we treat them in that order.

a. The servant should exercise the greatest care and self-denial in eating and drinking before the meeting. Many a good address has been heavy and powerless because the preacher was thoughtless or self-indulgent in this respect. If possible, walk to the meeting alone with the Lord Jesus.

b. In mental preparation each man must be a law unto himself. Few have attained to the spiritual stature of the late Lord Radstock, who once told me that he never prepared addresses but simply stood and spoke of what he was thinking about and enjoying. Those who heard that mighty Levite will appreciate the foregoing.

For myself, I always keep a piece of paper headed with the date, place and subject of each forthcoming meeting, and if I meet with anything in the course of my reading likely to illustrate or to be of service in developing my subject, I jot it down; and two days before the meeting I make a careful, word by word study of the passage, and then weave in any thoughts that have come to me, and finally write out the whole message.

While it is well to prepare carefully, let us beware of becoming slaves to paper. Personally I never refer to notes in preaching—I like to yield myself utterly to the guidance of the Spirit of God at the moment, allowing Him to lead along any bypath of thought that He may choose, quite careless as to whether I use the material which I may have prepared. Remember that a man is mentally and spiritually at his highest in the act of preaching, and when he is facing some hundreds of his fellows he is at that moment the chosen vessel for the conveyance of truth, and hence he is then specially responsive to the voice of the Spirit.

c. Perhaps the preparation of the spirit is almost too sacred for me to touch upon. At any rate a good rule is not to spend more time in speaking to the people than you have passed upon your knees. Also, do not leave your prayer time until just before the meeting, as it often takes time to get through, or as J. B. Stoney put it, to get an audience. May the gracious Lord bless each preacher and give us a rich harvest of souls.'

He spent a good deal of time writing, but it cost him much labor, and he never considered himself a writer. In South America he helped largely with the compilation of a Spanish Concordance for the Argentine. He wrote some of the adult Scripture Union Notes, and numerous articles, and published two books, *Behold My Glory, Studies in the Gospel of St. John* and *An Analysis of the Gospel of Mark.* These books appeal more to mystics and scholars than to the general public, although many of his readers would have welcomed more of his sensitive, detailed expositions.

In this way he passed most of the sixty years of his preaching life. Like the disciples of long ago, he took the bread of life direct from the hand of Jesus ("In the Father's house there is bread enough and to spare," he loved to quote in his prayers), and having gazed for a while into His face and received his supply, he would turn back radiant and satisfied to the hungry multitude and give that which had been broken and blessed by his Master. His type of ministry did not change much with the years, save that it deepened and mellowed. He was never particularly interested in stunts or programmes, nor did he attempt to keep up with the new, up-to-date styles of preaching. "I tend to remain a conservative in religious matters," he once said, "until you can present to me a better Bible than the one I know and love, and until you can present a better Saviour than the One Who died nineteen hundred years ago, and until you can present a better Father than the One I worship and to Whom I say, 'Our Father, which art in heaven.'"

CHAPTER 14

The Victor

THOU makest the outgoings of the morning and evening to rejoice." "It is easy to understand the outgoings of the morning rejoicing. You go to meet a new day full of hope and gladness; the sun is
shining and you are not surprised that they rejoice, but what about the
outgoings of the evening? It is good to go out on Saturday afternoon
when you are twenty, in the morning of life; you expect to rejoice. But
when a man is sixty or seventy, does God still make the outgoings of
the evening to rejoice? I expect many of us would rise up at once and
say, 'Certainly He does.' He not only gives bright light at dawn, but at
evening time there is light!'

> *Oh to go back across the years long vanished,*
> *To have the words unsaid, the deeds undone,*
> *The error canceled, the deep shadows banished*
> *In the glad sense of a new life begun.*
> *To be a little child whose page of story*
> *Is yet undimmed, unblotted, without stain,*
> *And in the sunrise of primeval glory*
> *To know that life has had its start again.*
>
> *I may go back across the years long vanished,*
> *I may renew my childhood, Lord with Thee,*
> *When in the shadow of Thy Cross are banished*
> *All other shadows that encompass me.*
> *And o'er the road that once was rough and dreary,*
> *My soul, made buoyant by Thy strength divine,*
> *Shall run the Heavenly Race and not be weary,*
> *Shall bear the blessing that has made me Thine.*

Mr. St. John loved to quote this poem, and the second verse certainly describes the last mellow years of his life.

In near Eastern countries there is about an hour, before sunset, when the light lies over the land with a last golden intensity never seen at any other time of day. The activities of nature have died down, and in the bright silence insignificant objects stand out with sudden vividness and the far distances are clear. The very air seems golden and the world transfigured, as though the day is pouring out all it has to give in a last abandonment of light. Sunset comes suddenly, but long after darkness has fallen the East still glows.

Harold St. John's old age reminded one of this. Those last years glowed with a peaceful joy, transfiguring his surroundings, investing every small incident with a new glad importance, lighting up life's values with holy clarity. He recognized this evening light and exulted in it, although weakness and limitation of service were new to him. Yet nothing was wrested from him forcibly. When the time came, he laid aside his duties with humble, yet noble dignity. One never sensed a negative void, but the positive peace of renunciation and acceptance, and this peace was breathed out in the many letters he wrote.

"What a relief it is," he wrote to one of his children, "that we do not build our nests in this death-doomed forest. At present the world is passing through a hurricane, but they are always short. Mother and I are very happy and quiet—the peace that broods over John 13-17 lies upon us. Christ Himself asked nothing from the world, as far as saving it was concerned, except a Cross on which to stretch Himself."

"I was struck today with the spiritual energy of Paul in Romans 15," he wrote to an old friend also experiencing the limitations of old age. "No letting up with the years, but abounding in hope through the power of the Holy Ghost. He knew that he was the prisoner of God's will—held by the power of God, not free to dispose of himself. The ram in Genesis 22 was caught by its horns in a thicket; it was not free, but marked for death. The colt was tied at the cross roads, held because the Lord had need of him. So, in a quiet way, of you and me."

He laid aside his traveling ministry gradually. He had long been warned that he must not walk long distances carrying heavy bags, but the life-long habit of fending for himself died hard. He had one or two alarming faints going up-hill, and at last his doctor persuaded him that his traveling days were over and his ministry should be relegated to nearer home—and he found a very real ministry right in his own home. Through the kindness of Miss Swain, his sister-in-law, Headmistress of Clarendon School, Abergele, Mr. and Mrs. St. John were able to live in a flat right on the school premises, and he shared the senior Scripture teaching.

"It was always a wonder to me, on looking back, that such a scholar should bother to teach schoolgirls," wrote a sixth former of that time. But bother he certainly did! He prepared those lessons with as much conscientious thoroughness as though he were digesting the subject matter for the first time. Long before each lesson he could be seen pacing up and down the main hall or the forecourt, his Bible under his arm, communing with God. And when he entered the classroom, an atmosphere of expectancy would prevail as the old white-haired teacher opened his book.

He had an engaging, half humorous way with him which won the confidence of his scholars, and they would often seek him out and talk freely with him. His opening prayer, never more than a sentence or two long, or his introductory remark usually arrested the most wandering attention.

"We have just finished the book of Ezra, and we are now going to study the book of Nehemiah," he remarked brightly at the beginning of a lesson, "and the difference between them was this—Ezra tore out his own hair, Nehemiah tore out other people's."

"In taking up the history of Jacob," he explained, by way of introduction, "we must realize that when God wants to crown a man He always cripples him first. The greatest men of the Bible limped to heaven."

Many are the letters from parents and girls that testify to the lifelong formative value of those deep, sane, human expositions of Scripture. "I have such wonderful memories of Mr. St. John walking up and down the forecourt meditating just before a Scripture lesson. The book of Job first lived to me through those lessons," wrote one.

"I always remember him standing with his face shining as though reflecting the light of the Lord as he gave those Bible studies," wrote a foreign member of the staff.

"Those of us privileged to have had a daughter at Clarendon feel we owe him a special debt of gratitude," wrote a parent. "Perhaps we can never fully know all that his spiritual influence and teaching has meant to the young people, but we do know that he has done much to build up their faith and strengthen their footsteps on the heavenly pathway."

Between Mr. St. John and his sister-in-law, whose loving kindness had followed him and the family all down the years, there existed the closest possible friendship. He had watched the growth of her school with deep, prayerful interest, and now he rejoiced in this new ministry. "4A are such lambs!" he would remark exultantly after forty minutes spent with a particularly lively group of fourteen and fifteen year olds. "We have such interesting discussions!" And even the younger children found him extraordinarily approachable. They would sometimes come to him with their small troubles and tears, and more often with hot faded bunches of flowers or little home-made gifts. For his last Christmas they made him a tiny Christmas tree, decked with presents, and he sat proudly in the shade of it for weeks after.

And now at least he had leisure to enjoy the things for which he had had but little time before—a quiet, peaceful home life, his grandchildren, the realization of the lasting love of his friends and, most of all, the gradual dawning consciousness that he would soon see the Lord. These were some of the ingredients of his deep, tranquil content.

In bearing and character he seemed a part of the gracious old house with its stately staircase and the mellow beauty of its panelling. The space and dignity of the place suited him, and he loved to pace the wide main corridors, meditating, his silver head bowed, his book under his arm. He spent hours in his study, too, and his commentary on Mark and an unfinished commentary on Ephesians were written during the last two or three years of his life.

But to him, the heart of the whole place was the little sitting-room in the flat where in the evenings he would sit resting with his wife, talking over his next day's lessons, sharing the family letters, or chatting about his children. Sometimes he would look back reminiscently like a traveler nearing a summit; and the path behind him, as he saw it, was sunlit all the way.

"Take plenty of time for rest and quiet," he wrote to his wife, "and keep a good wide margin for giving thanks for the children. We have been so terribly happy in all five and in the three daughters-in-law. You met me at the foot of the hill, and I am nearly at the top, but oh! what a lovely climb it has been, and what a world of wealth and music they have brought us—and what a joy that we are all, without exception, one in Christ Jesus."

"Christ fold you in His care," he wrote to one of his children. "Many things lessen with me now, but the firm deep grasp of my love for you all stands as tenacious and satisfying as ever. Indeed, it grows."

There was the new delight of a whole flock of little grandchildren. He did not live to see them all, but eight were born in the last ten years of his life and he frankly doted on them. He came out to Morocco in 1952 and rejoiced over tiny Paul, the eldest of his eldest son; and those in England frequently paid him visits. It was a pleasant sight to see him sally forth through the front gates hand in hand with Hugh, age two, to spend half an hour together on the seesaw. Such was his liking for Hugh that he had his cot placed beside his own bed at night, and one evening Hugh stretched further than his grandfather had imagined possible, and got hold of a file of hundreds of loose Bible Study papers, all carefully arranged in alphabetical order, and scattered them like Autumn leaves all over the floor. His parents were horrified, but the infatuated grandfather thought it very funny and rather clever, and laughed till his sides ached at the golden-haired rascal in a flannel nightgown who peeped roguishly over the edge of the cot.

Michael was a rather gentler character, and "Jampa," as he called Mr. St. John, was his ideal. The following conversation was overheard between Michael, aged four and his sister Hazel, aged five.

Hazel: "You be the doctor and I'll be the nurse."

Michael: "No. I'm Jampa."

Hazel: "Well you be a man, and I'll be a fairy."

Michael: "No, I'm Jampa."

Hazel (exasperated): "Well, Michael, you know you are not really Jampa."

The thoughtful devotion of such a little child was unusual and touching. Michael often came up to Abergele with his father for the weekend when Mr. St. John was really ill and nearing the end of his life, and the tiny boy would lean his head on his grandfather's pillow and sit quiet as a mouse keeping silent company. In the morning his first anxious question on awaking would be, "Do you think Jampa has had a good night?"

Mr. St. John dedicated five of his eight oldest grandchildren to the Lord, and the very last public service he performed was the dedication of Evelyn, aged three weeks old, brought from Coventry by her parents for the occasion. It took place in the sitting-room of Mr. St. John's home, and a few near friends were invited. Perhaps he knew that for him the end was not far off, for he made a very solemn appeal to the parents and all present to dedicate themselves afresh to God for the sake of that little child. "As Hannah and Mary presented their firstborn, I beseech you, by the mercies of God, present your bodies a living sacrifice, holy, acceptable unto God."

It was also forced upon his consciousness, during those last years, how much and how widely he was beloved. His innate humility had always repudiated the idea, but now he realized that there was no falling off of friendship with old age, and the presentation made by a group of leading brethren on his 75th birthday amazed and delighted him. It was staged as a complete surprise after he had conducted the wedding of Mary Price, the daughter of Mr. George Price, one of his oldest, closest friends. He wrote the following letter in reply.

> My dear friends,
>
> I cannot possibly express in words the surprise and pleasure that your remembrance of my 75th birthday has brought me. The presentation was made at Mr. George Price's house on Saturday last.
>
> The gifts themselves are exactly what I was needing—for my comfort, a real camel hair dressing gown; for my travels, a very light leather traveling bag; for my pocket, eight pounds in notes; for my intellect, Huck's Greek harmony of the Gospels; for my spirit, Souter's most recent edition of the New Testament, and for my heart, the restful gladness of knowing that I have a niche in the memory and in the affection of 53 such friends.
>
> It is 57 years since the Lord laid His hand on me for the ministry. The generous fellowship of countless Brethren in six continents has never flagged. The patient wisdom and care of my Lord has never failed me, and while I have nothing to say as to the quality and quantity and texture of my service, there is no question as to the reality of the call.

The twilight of my life is a very sacred and delightful experience. The Book I have loved and lived by yields its secrets to me far more fully than ever before, and the face of the Lord is brighter. The companionship of my dear wife, my sons and daughters, and the value of your friendships make it possible to say that 'at evening time it shall be light.'

Separated from his friends, in an isolated part of the British Isles, his heart overflowed toward them, spanning the distances; and from all over the world, from homes that had been blessed by his presence, from conference centers where he had ministered in the fullness of the Spirit, came greetings, and tributes and heartfelt sorrow that he would never again visit them.

"I could easily weep as I think of you," wrote an old man whom Mr. St. John had taught as a boy, "but you have never inspired weeping, but praising. I thank God on every remembrance of you and find myself checking some untoward thought or impulse or making some decision, as a result of recalling some word of yours or from just remembering you. Your influence has been beyond all ken."

It was with real sadness that he realized in April, 1956, that he would never again lecture at his beloved South Park Chapel, and they, who had so deeply valued his ministry for so many years, felt they could not let the accustomed month pass without some message. In reply to their request he sent the following letter.

For so many years I have come to you that it is a deep deprivation not to visit you this year. I imagine myself looking down on you from the familiar pulpit at South Park Chapel. Some of us are ageing and life leaves its mark upon us, but some of you, thank God, are still young. What shall I say to you?

Firstly, to those who are older: I can bear witness that there is light at eventide, and the lamps shine brightly at dusk. He who has supplied the needs of life can not, and will not fail (Joshua 23:14).

Secondly, to my youngers I would say three things:

a) Never accept a cheap salvation, but take your share of hardship for Christ's sake. Keep faith with God in such matters as the morning watch, and be regular and orderly in your Bible reading. Never let a day pass without getting fresh manna from the Book. Learn to watch for souls and to fish for men.

b) Keep the door of your lips. Read and ponder James 3. Much of the weakness in the Church and the barrenness of the mission field are due to careless talking. Nothing forfeits the respect of the wise like that.

c) Never allow depression to invade your life. God has planned that all things shall head up in Christ. His coming is as sure as the dawn. He will not fail or be discouraged. Never kill time, but always redeem it. Decide before God what is His will for you in recreation, music, games, general reading, or whatever it may be, and keep within your ration. Give to the needy and to the work of God generously and wisely. You are not your own; your life is a loan from God. Cultivate a hunger for holiness and learn to love the unlovely.

A personal word in closing. I am well, with no aches and pains, but a small reserve of strength. I speak a little at the meeting and teach a few senior classes of girls. I have you all in my heart. The Book yields more than ever it did, and the gladness of God is greater than I've ever known. The Lord bless, keep, and sanctify you all (1 Thes. 5:23).

And to one with whom he would no longer share the pulpit, he wrote:

"My love and confidence have gone out to you for many years, and I have watched the growing of your powers of ministry and of your increase in the grace of God. As shades of evening gather around us old folk, the certainty that God is raising up those who will carry on the doctrine and the tradition more ably than we have done is an ingredient in our happiness as we move off the stage."

And how he exulted in the sentence, "At evening time it shall be light." He had never feared the last shadows, and as physical weakness became marked he wrote to Mr. Balloch, "You and I have found that at eventide it is still light. If shadows come, and mental powers crumble, I think there will always be a response when the name of Jesus is sounded."

In fact he was forearmed. He had often looked quietly forward with a sort of eager, fearless curiosity to that last mile and had wondered by what route he would go home. He had spoken of this hope long before in a lecture on John 21.

"There is Christ walking on, on, into eternity, and by His side there walks one man. He is going to die, and at his heels there is another man, who, if Christ will, may tarry till He comes. So there are two highways by which all men shall leave this world; either by the lower road of death, or by the upper road of tarrying; and with all my heart I hope I shall be among those who tarry. I am ready to die, by the mercy of God. It would be a great experience, and in some ways I would not miss it for a lot—to go down into the valley of the shadow of death and have Christ with me, that is good. But there is something better, and that is, not to die at all, but to hear the shout which may be tonight. I long to see Him!"

For beyond the valley he knew that he would see Christ, and that light streamed across the shadows so that the pathway ahead looked bright till the end. In fact, he often forgot the path in the joy of the destination.

"So the believer on the journey of life," he once said, "may meet adversity or prosperity, sorrow or joy, temptation or triumph; but amidst them all he quietly whispers to himself, 'I am a son of God.' And, waiting for the end, he knows that behind the gates of death or glory Christ is standing, and He holds the keys to all the mysteries of life."

And near the end he wrote, "For myself, I am rejoicing in the sentence, 'The Lord shall preserve thy going out.' Out, from a world rent and saddened by strife, yet brightened everywhere by the faces of men, women and children who love Jesus. And 'thy coming in'; the land we are going to is so beautiful that I wonder why the Lord keeps so many of us here. He must need us for some task. But when we enter in there will be no shadows."

He was always an intensely happy man, and when, during the last months of his life, his heart condition gradually became more severe, and he became bedridden, his quiet joy never lessened. "I can never hope for any change now except the great one, can I?" he asked rather wistfully after a visit from the doctor. And having fully realized that, humanly speaking, no further improvement could take place, he quoted quietly, "I have seen an end of all perfection: but Thy commandment is exceeding broad." And a little later he asked his daughter to read him the story of Barzillai: "Let Thy servant go but a little way over Jordan."

The last eight months were weary ones. He had frequent heart attacks and could often only draw breath with oxygen, yet he never once complained or showed any impatience. His wife and younger daughter nursed him, and he was always thinking out little ways of sparing them, anxious for their rest, grateful, selfless, and utterly peaceful as long as one of them was near at hand. And all the time he was really ill, his wife practically never left the house.

Occasionally visitors were allowed in, and they always left the room with a wonderful sense of blessing. "I am so glad I was privileged to have that last talk with him on Confirmation Day," wrote the clergyman who had prepared the girls for their confirmation. "As usual, he was not thinking of himself, but others, and that was partly the secret of his joy which was so characteristic. Jesus Himself took the first place, others next, and himself always last."

Could that characteristic joy stand firm against the onslaught of increasing weariness, weakness and final helplessness? It did, and that quiet room was often a very merry place, for he never lost his sense of humor and would frequently murmur little jokes into the oxygen mask. And as his physical strength grew less, so his sense of Christ's presence and his power in prayer seemed to increase, and in spite of breathlessness he insisted on praying aloud daily in long, loving detail for the absent members of the family and the needs of the school. He was rejoicing in the hope of seeing his two eldest from abroad in July, but when he realized that he would probably not be here in July he accepted that, too.

"Tell them that the physical did not really matter," he said. "They were part of my life, and I've held them in my heart and prayed for them for forty years. They may be at the other end of the world but they are here all the time."

He spent hours in prayer and could often be heard in the night watches pouring out his heart to God. He read the papers till nearly the end and the needs of the world burdened him deeply. "Oh Lord, some of Thy people are so simple, and some are so subtle," he was heard murmuring. "Grant that those who think they are arranging the world may walk with God."

His morning petitions, after restless broken nights, were bright with praise. "Cause us to hear Thy loving kindness in the morning, oh Lord," he prayed. "Most people seek pleasure at night and are grumbly and out of sorts in the morning, but we have started the day with Thy loving kindness. We are going out bathed with Thy loving kindness."

He longed to go, and often the one who watched beside him at night heard him praying to be taken Home. "We are nearing the end of our pilgrimage. . . . Now Lord, lettest Thou Thy servant depart in peace for mine eyes have seen Thy salvation. . . . Father I will that they also whom Thou hast given me be with me where I am. . . . Now Lord, what wait I for?" And on several occasions, when overtaken with a severe attack, he thought his time had come, and his face glowed with a sort of holy excitement. "Not victory, but triumph," he scribbled on a piece of paper when too breathless to speak; "a mere empty husk. . . all the victory with Christ."

Sometimes there were times when the physical struggle swamped all else, but even then his heart was anchored. "I feel like a little tug in a great storm," he gasped, "but I'm fastened to a great ship on ahead. It's going into Port. . . it can't sink and it can't lose its way."

His joy reached a climax during the last week of his life. "When I go in to see the King it will be bright, very bright," he murmured at intervals. "The King in His Beauty. . . pure, cloudless joy. . . it's all gone, all my sins, all my fears. . . only Christ now. . . I'm the happiest man alive. . . it's all bright, all bright!"

He expressed one wish two nights before he died. His son John had been in the habit of coming up from Coventry whenever possible at weekends, after finishing his practice. He would arrive during the evening, spend the early morning hours with his father and then return to work. On the Thursday Mr. St. John got confused as to the day of the week. "Isn't John coming?" he asked pitifully. Meanwhile, Oliver, his second son, who was much further away in Farnborough, had felt an urge to come at once and picked up John on the way. They were both sitting by their father's bedside when at 2 a.m. he woke again, fully alert and mentally clear. His face lit up as he saw them, and he was able to enjoy them both for about five minutes. Then he relapsed into the semi-consciousness from which he never recovered.

But he was still conscious of the presence of the Lord. While no longer recognizing those around him he was still trying to sing.

Jesus, my heart's dear Refuge,
Jesus has died for me.

At 2 p.m. on Saturday, May 11th, he suddenly looked up very steadfastly and stopped breathing.

Mr. St. John had dictated his own obituary notice some weeks previously and it was published in his own words, with the date inserted.

> Harold St. John, third son of Oliver Cromwell St. John, sometime Treasurer of Sarawak. A great sinner redeemed by the precious blood of a great Saviour. To be laid at rest in St. George's churchyard to await the coming of Jesus.

The funeral service took place in the little country chapel of Bodoryn amidst the buttercup fields. The few beautiful wreaths, and the hundreds of bunches of wild flowers picked by the children who loved him, spoke of his resurrection. The front of the chapel was a mass of bluebells, cowslips, may, primroses and young beech leaves, and three of his favorite hymns were sung, led by a choir from Clarendon School.

The funeral service conducted by Mr. A. J. Allen, Mr. G. C. D. Howley, and Mr. P. O. Ruoff, radiated his own joy. The chapel was filled with friends from far and near and Mr. Howley spoke of the many living men and women in many countries whose lives had been dedicated to God and transformed through Mr. St. John's ministry. His death had not interrupted his work; it was going on and increasing all over the world through his spiritual children, and he himself was serving more perfectly. There seemed no place just then for sorrow, only for praising, and a great crowd gathered round the grave to sing, "How good is the God we adore." When the guests finally separated there was a wide, bright rainbow spanning the sea.

"I've never been to such a funeral," remarked an old man from the village. "It was kind of joyful-like all the time."

Nor was it quite the end. One notice had gone astray, and a dear old friend from Rhyl never heard the news until the day after the funeral. But he set out alone by bus and climbed the hill and stood for a time by the newly covered grave looking back over the years and thanking God. Then he went home again to put down his thoughts on paper.

"There are changed lives and homes all over the world because of Mr. St. John," he wrote. "He was a kindly teacher and a gentle shepherd."

Hundreds and hundreds of letters poured in from all over the world, from high and low, old and young. Practically all spoke of his deep, strong influence, of the glad goodness that had so attracted. Hundreds wrote with a sense of real personal grief. "For us a light has gone out and the world is a poorer place," wrote the secretary of the North Africa Mission, who loved him as a father.

Yet, thank God, the light still shines, and the way is open to those who will follow. By steep, rugged pathways of obedience and self-denial, through the daily discipline of hard work and prayer, through belts of cloud where he still trusted and praised, he had climbed into the sunshine of the love of God where all the mists of gloom and depression and fear had been scattered. Not as a stranger he entered in when the time came, but as one who had long lived within sight of the gates and known afar off the face of the Redeemer and would fain have handed back the secrets of heaven which he had begun to discern so clearly while yet on earth—as he called once in his sleep shortly before he died, "I've found the solution to all our problems. It was love all the time."

Addendum by Hazel St. John

(Daughter of Harold St. John)

IT is a great joy to me that the life of my father, Harold St. John, is being reprinted by the newly established Kingsley Press. Many have spoken or written of the blessing they received through reading the first printing of this biography, which came out in 1961. It was written by my sister, Patricia, after our father's death in 1957. Harold's five children have now become 59 grandchildren and great grandchildren—scattered in different parts of the world, but mostly closely in touch. The older ones are grateful for the Christian heritage that is ours, and a number are in some form of Christian work.

After our father died in 1957, our mother went out to Tangier, Morocco, where Farnham and Patricia were medical missionaries. In the goodness of God, I was out there for a brief visit in 1976, taking a break from my work as a missionary teacher in Lebanon; and it was during my visit that our mother was taken home.

All five of Harold's children were saved in their youth and have maintained a consistent Christian testimony throughout their lives. Farnham, Patricia, and myself all served as missionaries on foreign shores; Oliver and John have both served God faithfully—one as a scientist and the other as a medical doctor.

From 1981 onwards Patricia and I lived together in Coventry, England, and Patricia continued her writing and her work with children until her death in 1993. Her books for children, teenagers and older folk are still being printed by Moody Press in the USA, and by Scripture Union and several other smaller publishers in Great Britain. Some of her stories are now in approximately 40 different languages. Two of her children's stories—*Treasures of the Snow* and *Tanglewood's Secret*—have been made into films; and a third, *The Secret of Pheasant Cottage,* is on the way. Letters still come to Patricia from grown ups and children in different parts of the world telling how they have found the Lord or been helped on in their Christian lives through her books.

Her autobiography, *Patricia St. John Tells Her Own Story,* was published soon after her death by Operation Mobilization.

My father's love for the Bible, his amazing knowledge of its contents, and his power to make it live are as relevant today as ever. His unfailing love for my mother and for each of us children and for so many friends throughout the world have left an indelible impression. I am grateful that the story of his life is again to be shared with others.

Like Enoch of old, Harold St. John walked with God, and I trust that the blessing he brought to others whom he met in his life time will be continued through the pages of this book.